THE GREEN BARBECUE

VEGAN & VEGETARIAN
RECIPES TO COOK OUTDOORS & IN

FOR PADMINI
SOME ALTERNATIVES
TO POTATO SALAD FOR YOU

THE GREEN BARBECUE

VEGAN & VEGETARIAN
RECIPES TO COOK OUTDOORS & IN

RUKMINI IYER

CONTENTS

I'm not sure there's anything nicer than cooking and eating outside. With good company, perhaps a dog or two, or even just contemplatively cooking a dish for yourself, it's incredibly satisfying to break cooking down into its simplest components – one heat source, and a bit of food. I'll often add a chopping board on a garden table to maximise my time outside, and with minimal fuss, and as much enjoyment as anyone could expect from a bit of lazy food prep in the sunshine, lunch or dinner rolls off the grill in courses, with nothing more from you than occasionally flipping something on the barbecue, drink in hand. As a patented oven-cookery enthusiast, in many cases I've given alternative indoor cooking instructions should you have inclement weather, live in a flat where barbecuing isn't practical, or feel like making the dishes at another time of the year.

Why a vegetarian book? As readers of *The Green Roasting Tin* will know, my family are vegetarian, and over the past few years most of my close friends have become vegetarian too. I myself eat meat very rarely, and it's the combination of flavours and textures in plant-based cooking that are of real interest, as that's what I cook for the people closest to me. The idea of an entirely vegetarian or vegan feast, packed with texture, flavour and colour, which opens up the world of cooking and eating outdoors to the people I love, is immensely appealing as barbecues are almost exclusively associated with carnivorous cooking – though this is something that is happily changing. I must namecheck one of my food mentors, Genevieve Taylor, whose vegetarian barbecue book *Charred* I have been dying to read, but refrained while writing, so as not to inadvertently cross over with the contents of this book. She is the queen of cooking outdoors – buy both, and double the number of vegetarian dishes for your barbecue.

Whether you're vegetarian – or indeed vegan, as more than half the recipes in this book turned out vegan almost by accident – or cooking for vegetarian and vegan friends, I hope this book will give you lots of ideas to maximise your time outdoors through the summer.

ABOUT YOUR BARBECUE

GAS OR CHARCOAL?

I have spent the last couple of summers (and one memorable winter – who says you can't barbecue in the snow?) cooking outside with a variety of barbecues. Expensive gas range? Check (although sadly not mine.) Inexpensive little gas barbecue, which took hours to attach to the gas canister, in the pouring rain? You bet.

And then charcoal, the messiest, most unpredictable, and my favourite. (Though I wish people would tell me when I've managed to smudge coal on my nose like an extra from *Mary Poppins*.) From set-ups not very much more complex than a tin bucket with a grill, which you'll see pictured in these pages, to a rather nicer Weber, a smart tabletop Heston and my much-loved little Prakti stove, most of the recipes in this book have been tested on a variety of different charcoal grills. My thoughts – which are entirely subjective – are below:

Gas: Couldn't be easier. The temperature of the grill will be stable throughout, you'll have an inbuilt lid, it's as controlled as cooking indoors. Downsides: you'll lose the smokiness and primal fire factor of cooking on charcoal or wood.

Charcoal: Pleasing caveperson + fire factor. The smoke will impart an incredible flavour to the food. You can use seasoned wood or dry garden twigs on the fire (eucalyptus, apple and plum are particularly nice) for extra flavour, or branches of rosemary, lavender or thyme. Lots of vegetables (aubergines, beetroot, potatoes, sweet potatoes) can go directly on the coals to cook, and more delicate things (tomatoes, feta, marinated black beans) can go on the coals in foil packets. Downsides: the temperature will vary through the lifetime of the coal, and until you get a feel for cooking on it (see overleaf) there's a risk your food will burn before it's cooked through, or just sit there getting smoked but not cooking at all. But I'd still rather have a go than not.

Charcoal tips: Use natural firelighters or a few twists of newspaper to get your coals going. Remember you need a decent airflow, so don't pack your coals too tightly in the barbecue. Once your coal – if it is good coal (see below) – starts turning white around the edges and the flames have died down, it's kicking off enough heat to start cooking something gently, so make the most of the heat and start within 10 minutes of lighting it. Your coals are at their hottest when glowing white, and if that is going to be too fierce for whatever you're cooking, use something suitably long-handled to bank them up on one side – this will be the hotter end, and you can cook more delicate food on the cooler side.

Note on charcoal: Please do try to buy sustainable British charcoal from well-managed estates, because cheap petrol-station charcoal has things in it that you don't want you or your family and friends to inhale. The Tregothnan estate in Cornwall, and Whittle and Flame do next-day delivery – their charcoal is easy to light, heats rapidly and you'll know you aren't creating an environmental hazard in your garden.

Lids: If your barbecue doesn't have one, you'll be unsurprised that I recommend a deep, inverted metal roasting tin; just be careful taking it on and off, and use heatproof gloves.

USEFUL THINGS TO HAVE

YOUR MINIMALIST OUTDOOR COOKING KIT CHECKLIST

GAS OR CHARCOAL BARBECUE + HEAT SOURCE

LONG-HANDLED TONGS
(and you only need one as – hurrah – everything is vegetarian)

LONG-HANDLED METAL FLIPPER

SMALL BOWL FOR OLIVE OIL

HEATPROOF (IDEALLY SILICONE) BRUSH to brush food with olive oil

COUPLE OF BOWLS OR ROASTING TINS to put cooked food in

BIG TRAY to put all of the above on

SLIGHTLY MORE MAXIMALIST IF PREPPING OUTDOORS

CHOPPING BOARD

KNIFE AND SPEED PEELER

COUPLE OF BOWLS for prepped food and vegetable peelings/scraps

AND IF YOU'RE GOING ON A PICNIC

KITCHEN ROLL. Lots of kitchen roll

SOMETHING TO SIT ON/EAT FROM AND DRINK OUT OF

WINE, WATER, SPARKLING WATER

DETTOL WIPES

OLD OCADO* BAGS to put rubbish in

*I jest. Any supermarket bag works.

SOMETHING TO START

SERVE PILED ON A PLATTER
OR HAND AROUND WITH DRINKS.

SOMETHING TO START

ROSEMARY GRILLED MUSHROOMS
WITH CRISPY HALLOUMI & LEMON

SPICED CHARRED BABY CARROTS
WITH HAZELNUTS & DILL (VEGAN)

GRIDDLED CHERRIES
WITH WARM GOAT'S CHEESE, MINT & WALNUTS

CHARRED ASPARAGUS
WITH CHILLI, PEANUTS & COCONUT (VEGAN)

GRIDDLED PINEAPPLE, HALLOUMI & MINT SKEWERS

JERK CAULIFLOWER WINGS
WITH BLUE CHEESE DIP

GRILLED WATERMELON
WITH FETA, CUCUMBER & MINT

SPICED PANEER KOFTE
WITH YOGURT & CORIANDER

CRISPY GNOCCHI – ON A STICK! –
WITH CHARRED PEPPERS & BASIL PESTO (VEGAN)

FETA & ALMOND STUFFED PADRÓN PEPPERS

ROSEMARY GRILLED MUSHROOMS
WITH CRISPY HALLOUMI & LEMON

I had intended to use rosemary branches as skewers for this dish, but this left me harrumphing in the kitchen with crumbled halloumi and rather bashed – if fragrant – herbs. Make your life easier and use bought skewers, chopping the rosemary for a marinade instead – less hassle, equally delicious..

Makes: 4
Prep: 15 minutes
Cook: 10 minutes

400g baby chestnut mushrooms
250g good halloumi cheese,
   cut into 2cm chunks
2 tablespoons chopped
   fresh rosemary
2 tablespoons olive oil
8 or so skewers, soaked if wooden

FOR THE DRESSING
2 tablespoons extra virgin olive oil
1 lemon, zest and juice
1 tablespoon chopped
   fresh rosemary
1 teaspoon freshly ground
   black pepper

Gently stir the mushrooms, halloumi, rosemary and olive oil together in a large bowl. Thread the mushrooms and halloumi alternately onto the skewers, working carefully so as not to break up the cheese.

Whisk together the extra virgin olive oil, lemon zest and juice, rosemary and black pepper, and set aside.

Once your barbecue is good and hot, grill the skewers for 4–5 minutes on each side, until the cheese is nicely browned, and the mushrooms are cooked through.

Arrange the skewers on a platter, pour over the dressing, and serve hot.

Note: If you can't get baby chestnut mushrooms, use halved ordinary chestnut mushrooms. You want the mushrooms a similar size to the halloumi, so quarter them if they're very large.

VEGAN

SPICED CHARRED BABY CARROTS
WITH HAZELNUTS & DILL

These spiced carrots are ridiculously moreish, to the extent that I've had to double up the recipe. Crushing your spices whole in a pestle and mortar makes all the difference to the flavour (I've been known to improvise by chopping them with a sharp knife instead) – worth trying if you have whole spices in, but alternatively, use ready ground.

Serves: 4
Prep: 10 minutes
Cook: 25 minutes

300g baby carrots
  or small peeled carrots
1 heaped teaspoon coriander seeds
1 teaspoon cumin seeds
1 teaspoon smoked paprika
1 tablespoon olive oil
½ teaspoon sea salt flakes

FOR THE DRESSING
1 tablespoon olive oil
1 tablespoon maple syrup
½ lemon, juice only
A pinch of sea salt flakes
10g fresh dill, roughly chopped
30g hazelnuts, roughly chopped

Parboil the carrots for 5 minutes to give them a headstart, then drain well.

Bash the coriander and cumin seeds in a pestle and mortar until coarsely ground, then tip into a bowl with the carrots, smoked paprika, olive oil and sea salt. Stir gently to coat.

For the dressing, mix the olive oil, maple syrup, lemon juice, sea salt, dill and hazelnuts together. Taste, adjust the seasoning as needed, and set aside.

Once your barbecue is at a medium heat, cook the carrots for 6–8 minutes per side, until just catching. You want them lightly charred and cooked through, so keep an eye on them and move them around as needed.

Once the carrots are cooked, tip them onto a platter and pour over the hazelnut dressing. Serve hot.

Note: If you don't have maple syrup in and you aren't vegan, you can use honey instead.

GRIDDLED CHERRIES
WITH WARM GOAT'S CHEESE, MINT & WALNUTS

In this dish, you heat the cherries through on the barbecue before tumbling them over warm goat's cheese with fresh mint and crumbled walnuts – an easy, elegant five-ingredient starter.

Serves: 4
Prep: 10 minutes
Cook: 15 minutes

200g fresh cherries, whole
150g goat's cheese log with a rind
2 tablespoons chopped walnuts
2 tablespoons chopped fresh mint
2 tablespoons extra virgin olive oil

Tip the cherries into the centre of a large piece of foil, then wrap it into a neat, sealed parcel, with the seam along the top. Place the foil packet directly on the coals (or on the grill if using a gas barbecue), and cook for 10–15 minutes, until the cherries are softened – they'll steam inside the packet.

Just before the cherries are done, place the goat's cheese log on the barbecue for 3–4 minutes, turning it every minute or so, just to warm it through. (The rind will protect it from the heat, don't try this if your cheese doesn't have one.)

Cut the warm goat's cheese into four equal pieces, and arrange them on your serving plates. Divide the hot cherries between the plates, then scatter over the walnuts and mint. Drizzle over the cherry juice from the foil packet and the extra virgin olive oil, and serve hot.

Cook indoors: Put the foil packet into the oven for 15 minutes at 180°C fan/200°C/gas 6.

CHARRED ASPARAGUS
WITH CHILLI, PEANUTS & COCONUT

Good, seasonal asparagus requires little more than butter, salt and lemon juice – but if you feel like changing it up, I love this lightly spiced version – the crunchy peanut and coconut work beautifully against the charred asparagus.

Serves: 4
Prep: 10 minutes
Cook: 10 minutes

500g asparagus spears,
   trimmed
1 tablespoon olive oil
A pinch of sea salt flakes

FOR THE DRESSING
50g salted peanuts
1 fresh red chilli,
   roughly chopped
1 teaspoon sea salt flakes
50g desiccated coconut
2 tablespoons olive or neutral oil
1 lime, juice only

Toss the asparagus spears, olive oil and sea salt flakes in a large bowl, and set aside.

Tip the peanuts, chilli and sea salt flakes into a pestle and mortar, then roughly pound them together until well broken down. Stir in the coconut, oil and lime juice, then taste and adjust the salt as needed.

Alternatively, if you don't have a pestle and mortar, finely chop the peanuts and chilli, then stir them through the other dressing ingredients.

Once your barbecue is good and hot, cook the asparagus for 3–4 minutes per side, until just charred and cooked through. Put the spears back into their bowl with the peanut and lime dressing, give them a good shake to get them well coated, then transfer to a serving platter and eat immediately – ideally with your fingers.

GRIDDLED PINEAPPLE, HALLOUMI & MINT SKEWERS

The *Flavour Thesaurus* advises readers to 'outsnoot the snobs' who disapprove of cheese and pineapple on a stick – they have complementary flavour compounds that make them a scientifically excellent match, as well as a nostalgic one. These skewers are an update on the classic, and the perfect way to kick off a summer party (for grown-ups).

Makes: 5 large skewers
Prep: 15 minutes
Cook: under 15 minutes

1 medium pineapple, peeled, cored
  and cut into 2½ cm pieces
225–250g halloumi,
  cut into 2½ cm cubes
1 fresh red chilli, thinly sliced
20g fresh mint, finely chopped
1 lime, juice only
Olive oil, for brushing
5 skewers, soaked if wooden

Tip the pineapple and halloumi into a large bowl. Mix the chilli, mint and lime juice in another bowl, then tip half the mixture over the pineapple and halloumi and gently stir.

If you have time, leave the pineapple and halloumi to sit for 15 minutes – if not, alternately skewer the fruit and cheese onto long wooden or metal skewers.

Once your barbecue is ready, grill the skewers for about 5–7 minutes on each side. You can brush the pineapple pieces with the oil if they start to look dry. Don't try to flip the skewers too quickly, or the halloumi will stick to the barbecue.

Once the fruit and cheese are nicely charred on both sides, remove to a serving platter, drizzle with the remaining chilli, lime and mint dressing, and serve hot.

Note: Cut your halloumi on the larger side, or it'll fall to bits when you try to skewer it. This recipe can be doubled or tripled as needed, or you can make it go a little further by dividing the amount above between 10 skewers rather than 5.

JERK CAULIFLOWER WINGS
WITH BLUE CHEESE DIP

An easy, moreish snack to hand around with drinks. I'd be tempted to double up on the dip, and use it the next day in sandwiches.

Serves: 4 as a snack
Prep: 10 minutes
Cook: 10 minutes

1 large cauliflower
2 tablespoons olive oil
1½ tablespoons jerk seasoning
1 teaspoon sea salt flakes

FOR THE DIP
100g blue cheese, crumbled
100g natural yogurt
25g mayonnaise
Freshly ground black pepper

Cut the cauliflower into medium florets, then put them into a large bowl with the olive oil, jerk seasoning and sea salt flakes. Mix well to coat, then set aside.

For the dip, stir the blue cheese, yogurt and mayonnaise together with the freshly ground black pepper.

Once your barbecue is good and hot, grill the cauliflower for 4–5 minutes per side, until charred and cooked through.

Scatter the florets with a little more salt as needed, and serve hot, with the dip on the side.

GRILLED WATERMELON
WITH FETA, CUCUMBER & MINT

A light, refreshing dish – perfect as a palate cleanser before moving on to the next round. Use your favourite type of melon – watermelon works well, but cantaloupe or galia are just as nice.

Serves: 6
Prep: 15 minutes
Cook: 15 minutes

1 small watermelon, quartered
   and cut into 1½ cm slices
250g feta
½ cucumber, halved and thinly
   sliced
Olive oil, for brushing

FOR THE DRESSING
2 tablespoons olive oil
½ lemon, juice only
A large handful of fresh mint,
   roughly chopped
1 teaspoon fennel seeds (optional)

Once your barbecue is good and hot, brush the watermelon slices with a little olive oil, and barbecue for 3–4 minutes on each side, until just charred.

If you're using a charcoal barbecue, wrap your feta in foil and place directly on the coals for 5 minutes per side to warm through – alternatively, place the foil packet on the grill for the same amount of time.

Mix the olive oil, lemon juice, mint and fennel seeds (if using) together. Once the watermelon is cooked, arrange it on a large platter. Scatter over the cucumber and crumble the feta into large pieces. Drizzle over the mint dressing, and serve warm.

SPICED PANEER KOFTE
WITH YOGURT & CORIANDER

These kofte are so addictive that I'm surprised they're legal – a crisp, just-charred exterior, meltingly soft inside, and perfectly spiced – well worth doubling up the quantities on this one, as between four, a platter of these will disappear very, very quickly.

Serves: 4
Prep: 20 minutes
+ 1 hour chilling
Cook: 10 minutes

1 x 225g block of paneer, grated
100g cold cooked potato, mashed
30g fresh coriander, chopped
1 teaspoon sea salt flakes
1 teaspoon ground cumin
1 teaspoon ground coriander
½ teaspoon ground turmeric
½ teaspoon chilli powder
1 teaspoon freshly ground
   black pepper
3 fresh curry leaves, chopped
   (optional)
1 tablespoon olive or neutral oil,
   plus more for brushing
1 free-range egg yolk
Natural yogurt and lime wedges,
   to serve

Mix all the ingredients apart from the yogurt and lime in a large bowl until thoroughly combined. Taste and adjust the seasoning as necessary, then using your hands, press the mixture into small oval kebab shapes as pictured – squeeze them really well so they compress, as this will help them stay together when cooking. Chill the kebabs in the fridge for at least an hour or overnight.

When you're ready to cook, wait until the barbecue is good and hot, then generously oil the grill – this will help prevent the kebabs from sticking. Grill the kebabs for 8–10 minutes, turning them gently every couple of minutes, until golden brown and crisp all over.

Serve as soon as they come off the barbecue, with yogurt and lime wedges alongside.

Cook indoors: Bake for 15–20 minutes at 180°C fan/200°C/gas 6 before finishing them off under a hot grill.

CRISPY GNOCCHI – ON A STICK! – WITH CHARRED PEPPERS & BASIL PESTO

Could I write a book without featuring crispy gnocchi? Of course not. So I give you my proudest barbecue creation. Forget about threading just plain old vegetables on a stick – here, you intersperse veg of your choice (I've done peppers here, but see the note below) on skewers with just-blanched gnocchi. The result is crisp perfection like you wouldn't believe.

Serves: 3–4
Prep: 15 minutes
Cook: under 10 minutes

1 x 500g packet of gnocchi
3 mixed peppers, chopped
   into gnocchi-size pieces
   (don't use green peppers)
2 tablespoons vegan basil pesto
3 tablespoons olive oil,
   plus more for brushing
A pinch of sea salt flakes
A good amount of freshly
   ground black peppercorns
8–12 skewers, soaked if wooden

FOR THE DRESSING
½ lemon, juice only
4 tablespoons vegan basil pesto
2 tablespoons extra virgin olive oil
A pinch of sea salt flakes

Tip the gnocchi into a bowl of just-boiled water, and leave to blanch for 2 minutes, then drain and run under cold water to cool.

Put the gnocchi into a large bowl with the chopped peppers, vegan pesto, olive oil, sea salt flakes and freshly ground black peppercorns, and mix well to coat. At this point you could refrigerate the gnocchi until you're ready to barbecue.

Thread the gnocchi and pepper alternately onto the skewers. Once your barbecue is good and hot, brush one side of the skewers with oil, then lay them over the barbecue at a slight angle (this stops them falling through) and cook for ßß4–5 minutes, until the gnocchi are crisp and brown. Brush the tops with oil, then turn over and repeat with the other side.

Meanwhile, mix the lemon juice, pesto and extra virgin olive oil with a pinch of sea salt flakes to taste. Once the skewers are cooked through, serve immediately, with the basil dressing alongside.

Note: There's really no limit to the number of things you could pair with gnocchi on a stick – try cherry tomatoes and halloumi or tofu, or cubes of fresh fennel and halved figs. And you could use red pesto or harissa or mustard mixed through with olive oil as a marinade.

FETA & ALMOND STUFFED PADRÓN PEPPERS

I love ordering Padrón peppers on the basis that 'some are hot, the others are not' (sounds better in Spanish) – though I have yet to come across a truly spicy one. While there's nothing like a round of barbecued peppers just by themselves, scattered with crunchy salt, these little numbers, each stuffed with feta and a plump almond, are a wonderful treat with drinks.

Serves: 4
Prep: 15 minutes
Cook: under 15 minutes

250g Padrón peppers
150g feta cheese,
   roughly chopped
A handful of unsalted
   blanched almonds
Olive oil, to drizzle

Slice through each pepper on one side, making sure not to cut all the way through. Stuff with a little feta – enough to fill the pepper and allow it to still close up nicely – and add an almond. Repeat until you've prepped the lot: at this stage they can be refrigerated until you're ready to barbecue.

Once your barbecue is good and hot, drizzle the peppers with a little olive oil, then transfer them to the barbecue. Leave them for 3–4 minutes until puffed up and blackened, then flip them over and cook on the other side for a further 2–3 minutes to finish.

Serve immediately with drinks (and a warning in case someone gets the mythical hot one).

Note: You could definitely do this dish with the colourful packets of mini-peppers that you sometimes see at the supermarket, but allow for a little more feta, as they tend to be larger than Padrón peppers.

FRESH & LIGHT

THE PERFECT COMBINATION OF GRIDDLED
AND CHARRED VEGETABLES COOKED ON THE
BARBECUE, FRESH LEAVES, HERBS, SALADY
BITS AND PUNCHY DRESSINGS.

PICK ONE OR TWO AS PART OF A SHARING FEAST
FOR A VARIETY OF TEXTURES, COLOURS AND
FLAVOURS.

FRESH & LIGHT

**GRIDDLED ASPARAGUS, RADISHES & BURRATA
WITH LEMON & BASIL**

**CARAMELISED MANGO
WITH SMASHED CUCUMBER, PEANUTS & LIME
(VEGAN)**

**HALLOUMI WITH RED PEPPERS,
ARTICHOKES & PRESERVED LEMON**

**GRAPEFRUIT & FENNEL PANZANELLA
WITH HONEY & WATERCRESS**

**CHARRED TENDERSTEM
WITH ORANGES, BLUE CHEESE & WALNUTS**

**GRIDDLED COURGETTE
WITH PARMESAN, ALMONDS & LEMON**

**GRIDDLED PAPAYA
WITH TAMARIND, CHILLI & COCONUT (VEGAN)**

**SUNSHINE SALAD: GRAPEFRUIT & AVOCADO
WITH ROCKET & POMEGRANATE (VEGAN)**

**SRI LANKAN-STYLE AUBERGINE STICKS
& PICKLED RED ONION (VEGAN)**

**BLACKENED PEPPERS
WITH WALNUTS, CHILLI & FENNEL SEEDS (VEGAN)**

**THYME-ROASTED CHERRY TOMATOES
WITH CORIANDER SEEDS & MOZZARELLA**

GRIDDLED ASPARAGUS, RADISHES & BURRATA WITH LEMON & BASIL

I love the combination of crisp and barbecued radishes against grilled asparagus, burrata and the crunch of good sea salt flakes. All this needs is a simple lemon and basil dressing, and you have a sharing platter that is both moreish and beautiful.

Serves: 4
Prep: 10 minutes
Cook: under 15 minutes

400g asparagus spears
200g radishes, half of them halved,
   the rest very thinly sliced
   (see note)
2 tablespoons olive oil
A pinch of sea salt flakes
1 burrata (about 150g drained),
   at room temperature
A handful of fresh basil leaves, torn

FOR THE DRESSING
3 tablespoons extra virgin olive oil
1 lemon, juice only
Sea salt flakes
Freshly ground black pepper

Trim the ends of the asparagus spears (or snap the ends off at the point where they break easily), then tip them into a large bowl with the halved radishes, olive oil and a pinch of sea salt, and mix well.

Put the thinly sliced radishes into cold water to crisp up. In a separate bowl, mix the extra virgin olive oil, lemon juice, a big pinch of sea salt flakes and freshly ground black pepper for the dressing. Taste and adjust the salt as needed.

Once your barbecue is ready, griddle the asparagus and halved radishes for about 6–8 minutes, turning them every so often, until nicely charred.

Transfer to a serving platter, scatter over the drained sliced radishes, and drizzle with most of the lemon dressing. Place the burrata in the middle of the dish and pour the remaining dressing over it, then scatter everything with the basil leaves and serve hot or at room temperature.

Note: When you prepare your radishes, halve the largest ones and slice the smallest ones, to make sure you don't lose any through the barbecue grill.

CARAMELISED MANGO
WITH SMASHED CUCUMBER, PEANUTS & LIME

This dish is fresh, light and everything you'd want from a grazing plate on a hot summer day. As a bonus, smashing cucumbers is very therapeutic.

Serves: 4
Prep: 15 minutes
Cook: 15 minutes

2 just underripe mangoes
1 tablespoon olive oil
1 tablespoon sugar
½ cucumber
20g fresh mint leaves
1 fresh red chilli, finely chopped
1 teaspoon sea salt flakes
1 lime, zest and juice
1 tablespoon olive or neutral oil
A handful of salted peanuts,
   roughly chopped

Cut the 'cheeks' off the mangoes, then halve each one so you have four quarters from each mango.

Once your barbecue is good and hot, brush the cut sides of the mangoes with the olive oil and scatter with a little sugar, then barbecue for 4–5 minutes per cut side, until you get nice caramelised char marks.

Meanwhile, cut the cucumber into 4cm logs. Pop them into a sturdy plastic bag, squeeze out the air, then give them a good bash with a rolling pin to roughly break them up.

Mix the bashed cucumber with the mint, chilli, sea salt flakes, lime juice and oil, then adjust the seasoning to taste.

Once the mango is cooked, arrange the pieces on a serving platter with the cucumber, drizzle any remaining dressing over the mango, scatter over the chopped peanuts and serve hot or at room temperature.

Note: You can gnaw the flesh off the mango stones so as not to waste it – just don't go near the bit where the stem meets the stone. It provides a similar sensation to eating kiwi when one is mildly allergic.

HALLOUMI WITH RED PEPPERS, ARTICHOKES & PRESERVED LEMON

Summer on a plate. After returning from Morocco, I started putting preserved lemons into everything – they work beautifully against the red peppers in this dish.

Serves: 6
Prep: 10 minutes
Cook: 20 minutes

6 pointy red peppers
A handful of fresh thyme
6 cloves of garlic
1 tablespoon olive oil
250g manouri, kefalotyri
  or halloumi cheese, sliced

FOR THE MARINATED ARTICHOKES
1 preserved lemon,
  finely chopped
1 lemon, juice only
1 x 280g jar of sliced artichokes,
  drained
2 tablespoons oil
  from the artichoke jar
A handful of fresh thyme leaves

Make a cut down the side of each pepper, and carefully stuff each one with a few thyme sprigs and a garlic clove.

To make the marinated artichokes, rinse the chopped preserved lemon well in a sieve (there's plenty of salt from the cheese, so you're taking off some of the brine). Mix with the lemon juice, sliced artichokes, artichoke oil and thyme leaves, and set aside.

Once your barbecue is at a medium heat, rub the peppers with the olive oil, and barbecue for 3–5 minutes per side before covering with a lid or an inverted roasting tin. Cook for 25–30 minutes, until soft.

Once your peppers are cooked, griddle the cheese for 2–4 minutes per side, until charred.

Arrange the peppers and cheese on a platter, and tip the marinated artichokes over the top. Serve hot or at room temperature.

GRAPEFRUIT & FENNEL PANZANELLA
WITH HONEY & WATERCRESS

Barbecued fennel is up there with making potato waffles in the toaster: an eye-opening food revelation. The fennel softens, sweetens, intensifies and crisps up – hands down my favourite thing to barbecue. Chop the bottom off, quarter the bulb, and you have a set of natural 'cups' which char into crisps – perfect by themselves, scattered with salt. Or you can add them to this grapefruit panzanella.

Serves: 4
Prep: 15 minutes
Cook: 20 minutes

4 mini or 1 large focaccia
1 large, round bulb of fennel
1 tablespoon olive oil,
    plus more for brushing
1 teaspoon sea salt flakes
2 pink or ruby grapefruit,
    quartered, skin on
1 bunch of watercress

FOR THE DRESSING
1 lemon, juice only
2 tablespoons honey
2 tablespoons extra virgin olive oil
1 teaspoon sea salt flakes

Preheat the oven to 180°C fan/200°C/gas 6. Tear or cut your focaccia into 2½ cm chunks and pop them onto a lined baking sheet. Bake for 20–25 minutes, until golden brown and crisp.

Prepare the fennel as described in the introduction, then tip the fennel cups into a large bowl with the olive oil and sea salt flakes. Mix to coat them evenly in the oil, adding more if you wish.

Once your barbecue is good and hot, barbecue the fennel cups in batches for 3–4 minutes on each side, until crisp and charred.

Brush the grapefruit wedges with a little olive oil, then barbecue for 3–4 minutes on each side, until just charred.

Whisk the lemon juice, honey, extra virgin olive oil and sea salt flakes together, then taste and adjust as needed.

Pile the watercress, fennel, grapefruit and toasted focaccia on a platter, and pour over the dressing, mixing lightly with your hands so everything is evenly coated. Serve hot or at room temperature.

CHARRED TENDERSTEM WITH ORANGES, BLUE CHEESE & WALNUTS

This is a simple, filling side dish: broccoli and blue cheese are one of my favourite flavour combinations, and work beautifully here with a touch of sweetness from the oranges and honey-lemon dressing.

Serves: 4
Prep: 10 minutes
Cook: 15 minutes

400g Tenderstem broccoli spears, blanched
Olive oil, for brushing
3 blood oranges or ordinary oranges, peeled and sliced
200g blue cheese, crumbled
A handful of toasted walnuts, roughly chopped

FOR THE DRESSING
2 tablespoons extra virgin olive oil
½ lemon, juice only
1 tablespoon honey
½ teaspoon sea salt flakes

Once your barbecue is good and hot, brush the broccoli spears with the olive oil and cook over a high heat for 4–5 minutes, until lightly charred. Turn them over and repeat with the other side.

Whisk the extra virgin olive oil, lemon juice, honey and sea salt flakes together for the dressing. Taste and adjust the lemon and salt as needed.

Once the broccoli is cooked, arrange on a platter with the orange slices. Pour over the honey dressing, scatter over the blue cheese and walnuts, and serve hot.

GRIDDLED COURGETTE WITH PARMESAN, ALMONDS & LEMON

This is a dish my sister used to make when we lived together, albeit she made it indoors in a griddle pan. It adapts perfectly to the barbecue – courgette really benefits from a good char, and the combination of Parmesan, almonds and lemon works beautifully. If you have some in the cupboard, finish this off with a drop or two of good truffle oil.

Serves: 2–4 as a side
Prep: 10 minutes
Cook: 10 minutes

3 medium courgettes,
   cut lengthways into ½ cm slices
Olive oil, for brushing
50g vegetarian Parmesan
50g toasted flaked almonds

FOR THE DRESSING
½ lemon, juice only
1 tablespoon extra virgin olive oil
1 teaspoon sea salt flakes
1 teaspoon freshly ground
   black pepper
A few drops of good truffle oil
   (optional)

Once your barbecue is good and hot, brush the courgette slices with a little olive oil, and grill for 3–4 minutes on each side, until just charred and cooked through.

Meanwhile, whisk together the lemon juice, extra virgin olive oil, sea salt flakes and pepper in a large bowl. Taste and adjust the salt and lemon juice as needed, and add a few drops of truffle oil, if using.

Use a speed peeler to shave long thin slices of Parmesan. Once your courgettes are cooked, gently tip them into the bowl with the dressing, and carefully turn them around until evenly coated.

Arrange the courgettes on a serving platter, scatter over the Parmesan and almonds, and serve hot.

GRIDDLED PAPAYA WITH TAMARIND, CHILLI & COCONUT

I've been known to serve this as part of a lazy brunch outside – the papaya only gains in flavour from a short stint on the barbecue, and works so well with a sharp tamarind dressing and a good shake of coconut.

Serves: 4
Prep: 15 minutes
Cook: 15 minutes

30g desiccated coconut
10g fresh mint leaves,
    finely chopped
1 fresh red chilli, finely chopped
30g tamarind paste, from a jar
    (not tamarind concentrate)
15ml olive or neutral oil
2 just underripe papayas, halved,
    seeds removed

Start by soaking your desiccated coconut in warm water for 15 minutes, then drain well. Mix with the chopped mint leaves and red chilli and set aside.

Meanwhile, mix the tamarind paste and oil together, and brush a little over the cut side of each papaya half.

Once your barbecue is good and hot, cook the papaya cut side up for 5 minutes, then flip and cook on the other side for 4–5 minutes, until it caramelises.

Serve the grilled papaya slices hot, with the remaining tamarind sauce and the coconut-chilli dip alongside.

SUNSHINE SALAD: GRIDDLED GRAPEFRUIT & AVOCADO WITH ROCKET & POMEGRANATE

Can you get more retro than grilled grapefruit and avocado? (Turn to page 30 to vote for cheese and pineapple on a stick, or alternatively, continue below.) Admittedly, the two feel pretty modern here – scattered with pomegranate, and served with a sharp mixed citrus dressing. A refreshing dish to serve on a hot day.

Serves: 4 as a side
Prep: 15 minutes
Cook: under 15 minutes

2 avocados, not too ripe
2 tablespoons olive oil
2 pink/ruby grapefruit, halved
1 bag of rocket (100–150g)
½ pomegranate, seeds only

FOR THE DRESSING
2 tablespoons extra virgin olive oil
½ orange, zest and juice
½ lime, zest and juice
1 tablespoon agave syrup
1 teaspoon sea salt flakes

Just before you are ready to barbecue, halve and stone the avocados. Brush them with the olive oil.

Barbecue the avocado and grapefruit halves for 4–5 minutes on the cut sides, brushing with more oil if needed.

To make the dressing, whisk the extra virgin olive oil, orange and lime zest and juice, agave syrup and sea salt flakes together, and set aside.

Once the avocado and grapefruit are lightly charred, remove from the barbecue and arrange with the rocket on a serving platter. Pour over the dressing, scatter over the pomegranate seeds, and serve hot.

SRI LANKAN-STYLE AUBERGINE STICKS & PICKLED RED ONION

After trying this Sri Lankan marinade for aubergines, I rarely want to eat them any other way – a perfect balance of chilli, vinegar and garlic along with other aromatics. The smoky charred aubergine works beautifully with them – and of course, you can make these in the oven if the weather turns.

Serves: 4
Prep: 15 minutes
Cook: up tor 15 minutes

3 aubergines, cut into 2½ cm cubes
1 teaspoon ground turmeric
1 teaspoon sea salt flakes
Skewers, soaked if wooden
Olive or neutral oil, for brushing

FOR THE ONIONS
100ml cider or white wine vinegar
1 tablespoon mustard seeds
1 fresh red chilli, finely chopped
1 clove of garlic, finely chopped
1 teaspoon caster sugar
1 red onion, very thinly sliced
Sea salt flakes, to taste

Mix the aubergine cubes with the turmeric and sea salt flakes in a large bowl, then thread them onto your skewers.

Once your barbecue is good and hot, brush the aubergines all over with the oil, then grill for 6–7 minutes per side, until charred and cooked through.

Meanwhile, tip the cider or white wine vinegar, mustard seeds, red chilli, garlic and sugar into a pan, and bring to the boil. Add the onion and a good pinch of sea salt flakes, stir well, then lower the heat, cover and cook for 15 minutes. The onions will soften and turn bright pink. Once cooked, taste and adjust the salt as needed.

Once the aubergine skewers are ready, pile them on a platter and dress with the pickled onions, reserving some if you wish to serve alongside. Serve hot.

Cook indoors: Pop the skewers into the oven for 30 minutes at 180°C fan/200°C/gas 6, until the aubergines are well browned and cooked through.

BLACKENED PEPPERS WITH WALNUTS, CHILLI & FENNEL SEEDS

There's a lovely Middle Eastern dip called muhamarra – roasted red peppers, walnuts and garlic blitzed together. This dish is a sort of deconstructed version of it, with the hot charred peppers torn into large pieces, and a moreish walnut, fennel and chilli pesto stirred through – a wonderful, filling side salad.

Serves: 4 as a side
Prep: 10 minutes
Cook: 20 minutes tops

3 whole mixed peppers,
  e.g. red, yellow, orange

FOR THE WALNUT PESTO
50g walnuts
1 teaspoon fennel seeds
½ clove of garlic
25g fresh flat-leaf parsley
65ml olive oil
½ teaspoon chilli flakes
1 teaspoon sea salt flakes
A squeeze of lemon juice, to taste

Once your barbecue is good and hot, place the whole peppers on the grill and char them on each side until blackened.

You can make the walnut pesto in a food processor, in which case blitz everything (except the lemon juice) together roughly, then taste and adjust with the lemon juice and salt (bearing in mind that the peppers have no salt, so a little more is fine).

Alternatively, if you don't have a food processor or feel like doing it by hand, finely chop the walnuts, fennel seeds, garlic and parsley together on a chopping board, then stir them into the olive oil with the chilli and sea salt and adjust the seasoning as above.

Once the peppers are soft and blackened all over, remove them to your serving platter. When they're just cool enough to handle, use a spoon to scoop the stem and seeds out, then tear them into large pieces. You can remove it if you prefer. You can also leave them whole as in the photograph opposite.

Stir most of the walnut pesto through the peppers, and scatter the rest over the top. Taste and add salt as needed, then serve hot or at room temperature.

THYME-ROASTED CHERRY TOMATOES
WITH CORIANDER SEEDS & MOZZARELLA

Think of this as a sort of hot caprese salad – by cooking the tomatoes in a foil packet on the barbecue with their vines, aromatic herbs, oil and salt, the flavours concentrate and intensify. They work beautifully against the mozzarella as you would expect, with added interest from the crushed coriander seeds – simple, yet luxurious.

Serves: 4
Prep: 10 minutes
Cook: 30 minutes

300g cherry tomatoes with vines
1 tablespoon olive oil
A few sprigs of fresh herbs
   of your choice – thyme,
   oregano, rosemary or basil
1½ teaspoons sea salt flakes
1 ball of mozzarella,
   at room temperature
1 tablespoon coriander seeds,
   lightly crushed
Freshly ground black pepper
1 tablespoon extra virgin olive oil
A handful of fresh basil leaves,
   to serve

Take a large piece of foil and tip your cherry tomatoes, their vines, the olive oil, herbs and 1 teaspoon of sea salt flakes into the centre. Wrap it up like a parcel, with the seams at the top, then place the foil packet directly on the coals for 30 minutes or on the grill if you are using a gas barbecue.

Once the tomatoes are cooked, tip them onto a serving platter along with all their juices. Discard the vines, then lay the mozzarella in the middle of the dish. Scatter the mozzarella with the crushed coriander seeds, ½ teaspoon of sea salt flakes and some freshly ground black pepper, and drizzle with the extra virgin olive oil.

Roughly tear the basil leaves, scatter them over everything, and serve hot or at room temperature.

Cook indoors: Put the foil packet into the oven for 30 minutes at 180°C fan/200°C/gas 6, until the tomatoes are softened and cooked through.

SOMETHING SUBSTANTIAL

HEARTY HERO VEGETABLES, ROBUST
ENOUGH TO TAKE CENTRE STAGE.

CARB IT UP

Big veg, big flavours. Potatoes, sweet potatoes, squash
(an honorary carb in my book).

**RICOTTA WITH GRIDDLED SQUASH, CHARD
HONEY & HAZELNUTS**

**GUNPOWDER POTATOES WITH FENNEL SEEDS,
CHILLI, CORIANDER & CASHEWS (VEGAN)**

**SWEET POTATOES
WITH ROSEMARY, LEMON & BLACK BEANS**

**SIMPLY BARBECUED NEW POTATOES WITH
TARRAGON, PEANUTS & CHIPOTLE (VEGAN)**

**SQUASH WITH CHARRED CARROTS, RED ONIONS,
CORIANDER SEEDS, PISTACHIOS & LIME (VEGAN)**

**CHERMOULA-DRESSED SWEET POTATOES
& SHALLOTS WITH POMEGRANATES & MINT (VEGAN)**

**SESAME CHARRED SQUASH WITH TENDERSTEM,
SPRING ONIONS, ORANGE & GINGER (VEGAN)**

**MOROCCAN GRIDDLED POTATOES WITH OLIVES,
CHICKPEAS & PRESERVED LEMON (VEGAN)**

RICOTTA WITH GRIDDLED SQUASH, CHARD, HONEY & HAZELNUTS

This is a really elegant sharing platter – let everyone help themselves to a scoop of ricotta along with the crisp, caramelised squash and charred chard (as it were). If you're having trouble finding chard, you can substitute asparagus in season, or Tenderstem broccoli.

Serves: 4
Prep: 15 minutes
Cook: 50 minutes

600g squash, cut into 2½ cm slices (no need to peel)
200g Swiss or rainbow chard
2 teaspoons olive oil
1 teaspoon coriander seeds, crushed
2 teaspoons smoked paprika
1 teaspoon sea salt flakes

FOR THE DRESSING
2 tablespoons extra virgin olive oil
1 tablespoon honey
½ lemon, juice only
A pinch of sea salt flakes

TO SERVE
250g ricotta
50g hazelnuts, toasted

Tip the squash and chard into a large bowl, and mix with the oil, spices and sea salt flakes.

In a separate bowl, mix the extra virgin olive oil, honey, lemon juice and sea salt flakes to make the dressing. Taste and adjust the salt as needed, and set aside.

Once your barbecue is good and hot, lay the chard on the grill and cook for 3–5 minutes per side, until charred and cooked through. Transfer to a platter.

Once your barbecue is at a medium heat, lay on the squash slices and cook for 25 minutes on each side, covered with a roasting tin or the lid.

Once the squash is cooked through, arrange on a platter with the chard, leaving space for the ricotta in the centre. Invert the ricotta, scatter everything with the hazelnuts, pour over the dressing, and serve hot.

GUNPOWDER POTATOES WITH FENNEL SEEDS, CHILLI, CORIANDER & CASHEWS

This might be one of my favourite dishes – beautifully spiced potatoes with crisp cashews, sharp with lemon. Consider doubling the quantities if you're inviting potato fiends over, or, like the family in *The Tiger Who Came to Tea*, you'll have none left. This is also wonderful with a tablespoon of butter added just before serving and a handful of off-piste grated cheddar (for non-vegans).

Serves: 4 as a side
Prep: 15 minutes
Cook: 1 hour

600g small roasting potatoes,
   e.g. Albert Bartlett Apache, halved
5 tablespoons olive or neutral oil
2 cloves of garlic, grated
2½ cm fresh ginger, grated
½ teaspoon fennel seeds, crushed
1 teaspoon coriander seeds,
   crushed
1 teaspoon black peppercorns,
   crushed
1 teaspoon cumin seeds, crushed
½ teaspoon chilli powder
1½ teaspoons sea salt flakes
1 red onion, thickly sliced
1 teaspoon ground cumin
1 teaspoon ground coriander
1 lemon, juice only
1 fresh red chilli, thinly sliced
A big handful of fresh coriander
   leaves
50g cashews, toasted

Tip the halved potatoes into a large bowl with 3 tablespoons of the olive or neutral oil, the garlic, ginger, crushed spices (you can do these in a pestle and mortar or spice grinder), chilli powder and a teaspoon of sea salt flakes. Mix well.

In a separate bowl, mix the onion, ground cumin, ground coriander, the remaining 2 tablespoons of oil, the juice of ½ the lemon and another ½ teaspoon of sea salt flakes. Pile the mixture into the middle of a decent sized bit of foil, and make a neat parcel with the seam on top. Set aside.

Once your barbecue is ready, lay the potatoes on the grill, cut side down, and cook covered for 20–30 minutes. Turn them over, lay the foil packet on the grill, and cook both for a further 20–30 minutes, until the potatoes are cooked through and the onions are tender.

Mix the onions and potatoes in a serving dish, adding the spiced oil from the foil packet, and mix in the chilli, the rest of the lemon juice and the coriander leaves. Taste and adjust the salt as needed, then scatter over the cashews and serve hot.

SWEET POTATOES
WITH ROSEMARY, LEMON & BLACK BEANS

Baking sweet potatoes whole in their jackets intensifies and sweetens the flesh – one of my favourite ways to cook them. And, if you cook them directly on the coals, there's a wonderful smokiness on serving. I like to do this once I've finished barbecuing other bits and pieces, when there's still a good amount of heat left in the barbecue.

Serves: 6 as a side
Prep: 10 minutes
Cook: 45 minutes–1 hour

6 small sweet potatoes, whole
1 x 400g tin of black beans,
  drained and rinsed
1 lemon, juice only
3 tablespoons olive oil
2 sprigs of fresh rosemary leaves,
  finely chopped
20g fresh flat-leaf parsley,
  roughly chopped
6 tablespoons Greek yogurt

Place your sweet potatoes directly on the coals or on the grill if cooking on gas, and let them cook for 45 minutes to an hour, turning halfway, until completely soft all the way through.

Meanwhile, mix the black beans, lemon juice, olive oil, rosemary, and flat-leaf parsley in a bowl. Cover and leave to marinate.

Once the sweet potatoes are cooked through, dust off any coal, split down the middle, and stuff with the black bean mixture and a spoonful of Greek yogurt in each. Serve hot.

Cook indoors: Lightly oil the sweet potatoes and roast whole in the oven, on a lined roasting tin, for 45 minutes to 1 hour at 180°C fan/200°C/gas 6.

SIMPLY BARBECUED NEW POTATOES
WITH TARRAGON, PEANUTS & CHIPOTLE

The dressing for this dish is unusual – smoky chilli peanuts combined with tarragon – and somewhat addictive, especially when paired with crisp barbecued potatoes. You could easily use this as a dressing for grilled sweetcorn or mushrooms.

Serves: 4
Prep: 15 minutes
Cook: 30 minutes

600g new potatoes
2 tablespoons olive oil
1 teaspoon sea salt flakes

FOR THE DRESSING
10g fresh tarragon, leaves
  finely chopped
30g unsalted peanuts,
  finely chopped
3 tablespoons extra virgin olive oil
2 tablespoons lemon juice
A pinch of chipotle chilli flakes
A pinch of sea salt flakes

Boil the potatoes in salted water for 7–8 minutes, until just cooked through. Drain well, then mix with the olive oil and sea salt flakes.

Mix together the tarragon, peanuts, extra virgin olive oil, lemon juice, chipotle flakes and sea salt flakes to make the dressing. Taste and adjust the salt as needed, then set aside.

Once your barbecue is good and hot, griddle the potatoes for 5–8 minutes per side, until nicely charred.

Halve the barbecued new potatoes, mix with the tarragon dressing, and serve hot.

Note: If you have time, you can leave out the boiling stage and just cook the potatoes on the barbecue, in which case they will take about 1 hour.

SQUASH WITH CHARRED CARROTS, RED ONIONS, CORIANDER SEEDS, PISTACHIOS & LIME

A substantial and moreish main dish. The natural sugars in squash and carrots caramelise beautifully on the barbecue and work perfectly against the aromatic lime and spices.

Serves: 4
Prep: 15 minutes
Cook: 50 minutes

600g squash, cut into 2½ cm slices
    (no need to peel)
150g baby carrots, whole and
    unpeeled (or 3 medium carrots,
    peeled and halved)
1 red onion, quartered, core intact
2 teaspoons olive oil
1 teaspoon coriander seeds,
    crushed
1 teaspoon ground cumin
1 teaspoon sea salt flakes
50g pistachios, roughly chopped

FOR THE DRESSING
2 tablespoons extra virgin olive oil
1 lime, zest and juice
2 teaspoons coriander seeds,
    crushed
½ teaspoon black peppercorns,
    crushed
1 teaspoon sea salt flakes

Tip the squash, carrots and red onion into a large bowl, and mix with the oil, spices and sea salt flakes.

In a separate bowl, mix the extra virgin olive oil, lime zest and juice, coriander seeds, crushed black pepper and sea salt flakes. Taste and adjust the salt as needed, and set aside.

Once your barbecue is ready, lay the squash slices on the grill, and cook for 25 minutes on each side, covered if you can. The carrots and the onions should only take about 15 minutes per side, so pop them on 10 minutes after the squash and take them off 10 minutes before the squash.

Once the vegetables are all cooked through, transfer them to a platter and gently mix with the lime and coriander-seed dressing. Scatter with the pistachios, and serve hot or warm.

CHERMOULA-DRESSED SWEET POTATO & SHALLOTS WITH POMEGRANATES & MINT

Think about a good, fresh pesto, then think about it made with fresh coriander, mint, preserved lemon and warming spices. Voila! – you have chermoula, a North African herb-and-spice mix. It's wonderful as an accompaniment or dip for pretty much everything that comes off a barbecue, and particularly charred sweet potatoes and shallots, as in this recipe.

Serves: 4
Prep: 15 minutes
Cook: 50 minutes

4 small sweet potatoes, halved
8 echalion shallots, whole, unpeeled
2 tablespoons olive oil
A pinch of sea salt flakes

FOR THE CHERMOULA
15g fresh coriander,
   leaves and stems
15g mint, leaves only
1 heaped teaspoon ground cumin
1 heaped teaspoon ground paprika
3 cloves of garlic, peeled
2 tablespoons olive oil
A pinch of sea salt flakes
1 preserved lemon,
   or ½ lemon, zest only
   plus 1 teaspoon white vinegar
½ pomegranate, seeds only,
   to serve

Mix the halved sweet potatoes and whole shallots with the oil and sea salt flakes in a large bowl until evenly coated.

Once your barbecue is at a medium heat, arrange the potatoes and onions in their skins on the grill, and cover with an inverted roasting tin or the lid. Cook for 25 minutes, then turn them over and cook for a further 25 minutes, or until the sweet potatoes are cooked through, and the onions are soft.

Meanwhile, blitz together all the ingredients for the chermoula (or finely chop them by hand). Taste and adjust the salt and lemon as needed.

Once the sweet potatoes and onions are cooked, carefully halve the onions and slip them out of their skins. Arrange the vegetables on a platter with the chermoula drizzled over, scatter over the pomegranate seeds, and serve hot.

SESAME CHARRED SQUASH WITH TENDERSTEM, SPRING ONIONS, ORANGE & GINGER

I love the Asian flavours in this dish: the sweetness of the squash works beautifully with the sesame, orange and ginger.

Serves: 4
Prep: 15 minutes
Cook: 50 minutes

600g squash, cut into 2½ cm slices
200g Tenderstem broccoli,
  blanched
2 tablespoons sesame oil
2 cloves of garlic, grated
1 teaspoon sea salt flakes
½ teaspoon chilli flakes
½ teaspoon Sichuan peppercorns,
  crushed

FOR THE DRESSING
2 tablespoons sesame oil
½ orange, zest and juice
2½ cm fresh ginger, grated
1 tablespoon sesame seeds
½ teaspoon sea salt flakes
3 spring onions, thinly sliced

Tip the squash and broccoli into a large bowl, and mix with the oil, garlic, sea salt flakes, chilli flakes and Sichuan peppercorns.

In a separate bowl, mix the sesame oil, orange zest and juice, ginger, sesame seeds, sea salt flakes and spring onions. Taste and adjust the salt as needed, then set aside.

Once your barbecue is good and hot, lay the Tenderstem on the grill and cook for 3–5 minutes per side, until just charred and cooked through. Transfer to a platter.

Once your barbecue is at a medium heat, lay the squash slices on the grill, and cook for 25 minutes per side, covered with a roasting tin or the lid.

Once the squash is cooked through, arrange on the platter with the broccoli. Pour over the sesame dressing, and serve hot.

MOROCCAN GRIDDLED POTATOES WITH OLIVES, CHICKPEAS & PRESERVED LEMON

This dish is inspired by one of my favourite tagines, which we made in a field kitchen in the desert on location for a film shoot in the Sahara. Olives, preserved lemon and potatoes work beautifully together; along with the chickpeas, this is almost a meal in itself. Forgive the lack of chickpeas in the photograph – I forgot to buy them and couldn't bring myself to open the rather fancy jarred kind at my publisher's house.

Serves: 4
Prep: 15 minutes
Cook: 30 minutes

600g new potatoes
2 tablespoons olive oil
1 teaspoon ground coriander
1 teaspoon ground cumin
½ teaspoon ground turmeric
1 teaspoon sea salt flakes
A handful of fresh mint, to serve

FOR THE CHICKPEAS
1 x 400g tin of chickpeas,
   drained and rinsed
1 red onion, finely chopped
80g pitted green olives
1 preserved lemon, finely chopped
2 tablespoons olive oil

Boil the new potatoes in salted water for 7–8 minutes, until just cooked through. Drain well, then mix with the olive oil, ground coriander, cumin, turmeric and sea salt flakes.

Take a large piece of foil and tip in the chickpeas, onion, olives, preserved lemon and olive oil. Fold into a neat packet with the seams at the top.

While your barbecue is heating up, place the foil packet directly on the coals or on the grill if using gas. Once your barbecue is good and hot, grill the potatoes for 5–8 minutes per side, until nicely charred.

When the potatoes are cooked through, tip them onto a serving platter and halve them. Open the foil packet of chickpeas, and gently stir them through the potatoes. Taste and adjust the salt as needed, scatter over the fresh mint, and serve hot.

DAIRY-ISH

Feta, paneer and tofu – the paneer and tofu recipes are helpfully interchangeable, so you can veganise as you wish.

SRIRACHA GRIDDLED TOFU WITH PICKLED ONIONS, LIME & CORIANDER (VEGAN)

PANEER WITH HARISSA, GREEN BEANS, CHICKPEAS & LIME

CRISPY BARBECUE TOFU LETTUCE WRAPS WITH CASHEWS, CARROTS & NUOC CHAM (VEGAN)

VIETNAMESE GRIDDLED TOFU WITH TOMATOES & SPRING ONIONS (VEGAN)

CHARRED PANEER & FENNEL WITH CHILLI ALMONDS, LEMON & DILL

DILL-SOUSED FETA WITH BEETROOT, CUCUMBER, APPLE & WATERCRESS

SPICED PANEER WITH MANGO, AVOCADO, CHILLI & CORIANDER

GRIDDLED FETA, PINEAPPLE & BLACK BEAN TACOS WITH CHILLI & LIME

SRIRACHA GRIDDLED TOFU
WITH PICKLED ONIONS, LIME & CORIANDER

This is such a quick dish to throw together. Do watch out for the sriracha, as it varies in strength by brand – the tablespoon used below was fiery, so by all means adapt it to your palate.

Serves: 4
Prep: 10 minutes
Cook: 15 minutes tops

1 x 280g block of firm tofu
   (I like to use Tofoo)
1 tablespoon sriracha
1 tablespoon neutral or olive oil
1 teaspoon sea salt flakes
A large handful of fresh coriander,
   chopped

FOR THE DRESSING
½ red onion, thinly sliced
1 lime, zest and juice

Cut the tofu into four pieces lengthways, and place them in a bowl with the sriracha, oil and sea salt flakes. Turn gently to coat, and set aside.

Blanch the red onion in a small pan of boling water for 30 seconds before draining well. Mix with the lime zest and juice and a pinch of sea salt, and set aside.

Once your barbecue is good and hot, grill the tofu for 3–4 minutes on each side, until well charred. Serve with the pickled onions, coriander and a scatter of sea salt flakes.

PANEER WITH HARISSA, GREEN BEANS, CHICKPEAS & LIME

Bought paneer works perfectly on the barbecue – crisp and charred on the outside and, if you time it right, soft on the inside. This version, spiced with harissa and served with crunchy green beans and marinated chickpeas, is perfect with flatbreads alongside.

Serves: 4
Prep: 15 minutes
Cook: 20 minutes

1 x 400g tin of chickpeas,
   drained and rinsed
20g fresh coriander,
   roughly chopped
1 lime, juice only
2 teaspoons sea salt flakes
3 tablespoons olive oil
225g paneer, cut into 2½ cm cubes
150g green beans
1 heaped tablespoon harissa
Yogurt and flatbreads, to serve

Mix the chickpeas with the coriander, lime juice, 1 teaspoon of sea salt flakes and 1 tablespoon of olive oil. Taste and adjust the seasoning as needed, then cover and set aside.

Tip the paneer and green beans into a large bowl with the harissa, the remaining teaspoon of sea salt flakes and the remaining 2 tablespoons of olive oil, and mix well. Set aside until you're ready to barbecue.

Once your coals are good and hot, griddle the green beans for a few minutes on each side until charred and cooked through, then set them aside. Repeat with the paneer until crisp and charred – don't let it cook for too long, or you'll lose the softness of the inside.

Put the paneer back into the bowl with the leftover marinade and gently stir it through to coat.

Pile the green beans, paneer and marinated chickpeas on a platter, and serve with yogurt and flatbreads.

CRISPY BARBECUE TOFU LETTUCE WRAPS WITH CASHEWS, CARROTS & NUOC CHAM

This is a combination I first tried in Vietnam – nuoc cham is such an addictive dipping sauce that it's tempting to drink it straight up. If you can resist, save some and use it for your crispy tofu instead.

Serves: 4
Prep: 15 minutes
Cook: 10 minutes

FOR THE TOFU
280g firm tofu
   (I like to use Tofoo)
1 lime, zest and juice
1 tablespoon soy sauce
1 clove of garlic, grated
1 tablespoon sesame oil

FOR THE CARROT PICKLE
1 medium carrot,
   cut into matchsticks
1 tablespoon rice vinegar
1 teaspoon caster sugar
½ teaspoon sea salt flakes

FOR THE NUOC CHAM
1 clove of garlic, peeled
1 fresh red chilli, roughly chopped
2½ cm fresh ginger
1–2 tablespoons soy sauce
50ml water
½ lime, zest and juice

TO SERVE
1 small cos lettuce, leaves separated
A handful of toasted cashews

Cut the tofu into large cubes, and put them into a bowl with the lime zest and juice, soy sauce, garlic and sesame oil. Mix gently to coat, then cover and set aside.

For the carrot pickle, mix the carrot matchsticks with the rice vinegar, caster sugar and sea salt flakes. Cover and set aside.

To make the nuoc cham, put the garlic, chilli and ginger in a pestle and mortar, and bash into a paste. (Alternatively, grate all the ingredients into a jug.) Add the soy sauce, water, lime zest and juice, and taste. Adjust the amount of soy, water and lime as needed, and set aside.

When your barbecue is good and hot, griddle the marinated tofu for 2–3 minutes per side, until lightly charred and crisp. Scatter with a pinch of sea salt.

Arrange the lettuce cups on a platter and add a spoonful of carrot pickle to each. Divide the crispy tofu between the cups, scatter with the toasted cashews and a drizzle of nuoc cham, and serve the remaining nuoc cham alongside.

VIETNAMESE GRIDDLED TOFU
WITH TOMATOES & SPRING ONIONS

This is one dish that I didn't manage to try while in Vietnam, but ate instead at a very good Vietnamese restaurant in Chicago. It's a simple dish, packed with intense flavour from the tomatoes. In this version, I barbecue the tofu for extra flavour and texture.

Serves: 4
Prep: 15 minutes
Cook: 50 minutes

250g cherry tomatoes on the vine
1 tablespoon tomato paste
1 teaspoon sea salt flakes
1 teaspoon sugar
1 clove of garlic, unpeeled
280g firm tofu (I like to use Tofoo)
2 tablespoons sesame or neutral oil
1 teaspoon sea salt flakes
1 teaspoon freshly ground black
  pepper

TO SERVE
4 spring onions, thinly sliced
1 lime, zest and juice

Take a large piece of foil and place the cherry tomatoes, their vines, the tomato paste, sea salt flakes, sugar and garlic in the middle. Fold it up to make a neat packet, with the seam on the top.

Press the liquid out of the tofu, using your hands and a clean tea towel or kitchen roll, then cut it into 1 ½ cm deep triangles. Gently dress them in a bowl with the oil, sea salt flakes and pepper.

Once your barbecue is good and hot, place the tomato packet directly on the coals or on the grill if cooking with gas and set a timer for 15 minutes. Barbecue the tofu for 4–5 minutes per side, until crisp and golden brown.

Once your tomatoes are cooked, tip them into a bowl and squash them down with a wooden spoon. Gently stir through the crispy tofu, scatter over the spring onions and lime juice, and serve hot or at room temperature. (What you lose in crispness by letting the dish sit, you gain in flavour.)

CHARRED PANEER & FENNEL
WITH CHILLI ALMONDS, LEMON & DILL

In this dish, the lightly spiced paneer combines with crisp almonds and sweet, caramelised fennel – a lovely, elegant sharing plate.

Serves: 4
Prep: 20 minutes
Cook: 15 minutes

50g blanched almonds
1 teaspoon butter
½ teaspoon chilli flakes
A pinch of sea salt flakes
1 x 225g block of paneer
1 round fennel bulb
1 tablespoon olive oil

FOR THE SPICE PASTE
1 teaspoon fennel seeds
1 teaspoon coriander seeds
1 tablespoon olive oil
1 tablespoon sea salt flakes
1 tablespoon tomato paste

FOR THE DRESSING
½ lemon, juice and zest
15g fresh dill, roughly chopped
2 tablespoons oil
A pinch of sea salt
Freshly ground black pepper

Start by mixing the blanched almonds, butter, chilli flakes and sea salt flakes in a small lined roasting tin, and toast for 10 minutes at 140°C fan/160°C/gas 3 until just golden brown.

While the almonds are in the oven, cut the paneer into 4 rectangles. Roughly crush the fennel and coriander seeds in a pestle and mortar, then mix with the oil, sea salt flakes and tomato paste. Rub the spice paste all over the paneer, and leave to marinate for at least 10 minutes.

Meanwhile, cut the stem off the fennel, quarter it, then pull apart so you have a series of small cups. Mix them in a bowl with the olive oil.

For the dressing, mix together the lemon juice, dill, oil, salt and black pepper. Taste and adjust the seasoning as needed.

When your barbecue is good and hot, grill the paneer and fennel cups on both sides in batches, turning them over halfway. You want the paneer just charred but still soft on the inside, and the fennel cups cooked through and charring around the edges – about 2–3 minutes per side for the paneer if the barbecue is very hot, and 3–4 minutes per side for the fennel.

Pile the charred fennel and paneer onto a serving platter, pour over the dressing, scatter with the chilli almonds, and serve hot.

DILL-SOUSED FETA WITH BEETROOT, CUCUMBER, APPLE & WATERCRESS

If you're using a charcoal barbecue, this dish is perfect to make towards the end – tip your beetroot cubes into a foil packet with lemon, lay them directly on the coals, and let them cook. Of course, you could also pop your foil packet into the oven and have this as an accompanying salad to your barbecue – I find the combination of sweet apple, beetroot, cucumber and feta mildly addictive.

Serves: 4
Prep: 15 minutes
Cook: 1 hour

800g beetroot, peeled
    and cut into 1½ cm chunks
A pinch of sea salt flakes
Freshly ground black pepper
1 tablespoon olive oil
½ lemon, juice only
1 apple, cut into 1½ cm chunks
150g cucumber, cut into
    1½ cm chunks
1 packet of watercress
1 block of good feta cheese
25g fresh dill, chopped

FOR THE DRESSING
2 tablespoons extra virgin olive oil
½ lemon, juice only
A pinch of sea salt flakes
Freshly ground black pepper

Cook indoors: Put the foil packet of beetroot on a baking tray, and cook in the oven for 1 hour at 200°C fan/220C/gas 7.

Tip the beetroot, sea salt flakes, black pepper, olive oil and lemon juice – and the squeezed-out lemon half, if you like – into the middle of a large piece of foil, then carefully wrap it into a packet, with the seam at the top.

Place the packet directly on the coals or on one side of the grill if using gas, and let it cook for 45 minutes to 1 hour, until the beetroot is just tender.

Meanwhile, mix the olive oil, lemon juice, sea salt flakes and freshly ground pepper together for the dressing, and set aside.

Once the beetroot is cooked, stir it through the apple and cucumber with a third of the dressing. Scatter the watercress over your serving plate, and dress with another third of the dressing. Tumble the beetroot, apple and cucumber over the top.

Flash the block of feta cheese on the barbecue for 2 minutes per side (watching carefully to make sure it doesn't melt through), or under a hot grill for a few minutes, then lay it over the top of the salad. Drizzle with the remaining lemon dressing, scatter with the dill, and serve.

SPICED PANEER WITH MANGO, AVOCADO, CHILLI & CORIANDER

Middle Eastern dishes liberally use herbs in the way that we would use salad leaves, so if you like coriander, this is the dish for you. The sweetness of the mango against the avocado and lightly spiced paneer make this a substantial salad, excellent with flatbreads and yogurt on the side.

Serves: 4 as a side
Prep: 20 minutes
Cook: under 15 minutes

1 x 225g block of paneer,
  cut into triangles
2 tablespoons olive oil
1 teaspoon cayenne pepper
2 cloves of garlic, grated
2½ cm fresh ginger, grated
1 teaspoon sea salt flakes
1 lime, zest and juice
1 large, just underripe mango
1 large, just underripe avocado
Massive handfuls of coriander
  leaves

FOR THE DRESSING
2 tablespoons olive oil
1 lime, zest and juice
1 fresh red chilli, finely chopped
A pinch of sea salt flakes

Note: I am far too lazy to pick coriander leaves by hand, but as you don't want stalks in this salad, the easiest thing to do is to buy a living pot of coriander from the supermarket, and give it a haircut just below the leaves before serving.

Mix the paneer triangles with a tablespoon of olive oil, the cayenne pepper, garlic, ginger, sea salt flakes, lime zest and juice, and set aside to marinate at room temperature for 45 minutes, or overnight in the fridge.

For the dressing, mix the olive oil, lime zest and juice, red chilli and sea salt flakes, taste and adjust the salt as needed, then set aside.

Take the cheeks off the mango and halve each, so you have 4 long wedges. Just before you are ready to barbecue, halve and stone the avocado, then cut it into quarters. Brush the avocado and mango slices with another tablespoon of olive oil.

Once the barbecue is ready, cook the marinated paneer, avocado and mango slices for 4–5 minutes on each of the cut sides, brushing with more oil if needed. You'll want to take the avocado off as soon as you have a few char lines – they're at their best just warmed through. The mango benefits from a longer cook.

Once the fruit and paneer are nicely charred, transfer them to a serving platter and gently mix with the lime and chilli dressing and the coriander leaves. Taste and adjust the seasoning as needed, and serve immediately.

GRIDDLED FETA, PINEAPPLE
& BLACK BEAN TACOS WITH CHILLI & LIME

Was this dish another attempt to get cheese and pineapple out of the eighties and back into the mainstream? Potentially. But no one can fault the combination of hot griddled pineapple with chilli, feta and lime-marinated black beans. Serve with margaritas.

Serves: 4
Prep: 15 minutes
Cook: 20 minutes

1 pineapple, peeled, cored
   and cut into eighths
1 teaspoon chipotle chilli flakes
1 tablespoon olive oil
1 x 250g block of feta
A handful of fresh mint leaves, torn
1 x 400g tin of black beans,
   drained and rinsed
1 tablespoon extra virgin olive oil
1 lime, zest and juice
8 tortillas, warmed

Stir the pineapple slices with the chilli flakes and olive oil, and set aside.

Wrap the feta in a piece of foil with a few of the mint leaves. Tip the black beans, extra virgin olive oil, lime zest and juice into another piece of foil and wrap it up in a neat parcel, making sure both parcels have the seams on the top.

Once your barbecue is good and hot, place the packet of black beans directly on the coals or onto the grill if using gas. Pop the packet of feta on one side of the grill, then grill the pineapple for 4–5 minutes on each side, until just charred.

Once the pineapple is all cooked, tip the black beans into a bowl and stir through the rest of the torn fresh mint and crumble through the warm feta. Taste and adjust the lime juice as needed. Pile the pineapple onto a serving platter, and serve with the warm tortillas for people to make their own wraps.

QUICK PREP, QUICK COOK

Sweetcorn, aubergines, mushrooms – simple dishes with just a handful of ingredients.

**FIVE-SPICE AUBERGINE
WITH PAK CHOI & LIME (VEGAN)**

**BARBECUED CORN WITH A GINGER, PEANUT
& CHILLI DRESSING (VEGAN)**

**GRIDDLED PORTOBELLO MUSHROOMS & LEEKS
WITH TARRAGON & WALNUTS (VEGAN)**

BARBECUED CORN WITH SAGE & PINE NUT BUTTER

**OREGANO, PINE NUT & MOZZARELLA STUFFED
MUSHROOMS WITH CHILLI**

**GRIDDLED AUBERGINE WITH CUCUMBER,
WALNUTS & CUMIN (VEGAN)**

SPICED PARMESAN CORN WITH LEMON & MINT

**YUZU MUSHROOMS WITH CORIANDER & CASHEWS
(VEGAN)**

**HALLOUMI STUFFED AUBERGINE
WITH LEMON & OREGANO**

FIVE-SPICE AUBERGINE
WITH PAK CHOI & LIME

Chinese five-spice gives a wonderful earthy flavour to these aubergines – paired with crisp, charred pak choi and a light dressing, this makes an easy, flavourful platter.

Serves: 4
Prep: 15 minutes
Cook: 20 minutes

3 aubergines, cut into 1½ cm slices
3 teaspoons Chinese five-spice
1½ teaspoons sea salt flakes,
    plus more to taste
4 pak choi, halved
Olive or other neutral oil,
    for brushing
2 limes, juice only
A handful of chopped fresh chives
    or coriander

Toss the aubergine pieces, five-spice, sea salt flakes and pak choi in a large bowl.

Once your barbecue is good and hot, fish the aubergines out of the bowl, brush them liberally with oil, and barbecue for 3–5 minutes each side, until charred and cooked through.

Set the aubergines aside on a platter, then repeat with the pak choi for 2–3 minutes each side, until wilted and just cooked through.

Scatter the pak choi over the aubergines, dress with the lime juice, taste and add sea salt flakes as needed, then serve scattered with the chopped chives or coriander.

BARBECUED CORN
WITH A GINGER, PEANUT & CHILLI DRESSING

One of the most popular recipes in *The Green Roasting Tin* is the Indonesian gado-gado – crunchy potatoes with an addictive peanut, coconut and chilli sauce. It occurred to me that the dressing, slightly adapted, would work beautifully with grilled corn on the cob – and joy, it did! This is now a summer staple.

Serves: 6
Prep: 10 minutes
Cook: 20 minutes

6 corn on the cob
2½ tablespoons olive
  or neutral oil
1 teaspoon sea salt flakes
50g crunchy peanut butter
80ml coconut milk
30ml lime juice
1½ tablespoons soy sauce
2½ cm fresh ginger,
  finely chopped/grated
1 fresh red chilli, finely chopped
10g fresh chives, finely chopped

In a large bowl, evenly coat the corn with the oil and sea salt flakes.

Mix together the peanut butter, coconut milk, lime juice, soy sauce, ginger, chilli and chives.

Once your barbecue is good and hot, cook the corn for 4–5 minutes on each side, turning as each side grills, until the whole cob is evenly charred to your liking.

Serve the grilled corn with the sauce alongside, and let people spoon the dressing over.

Cook indoors: Roast the corn in the oven for 45 minutes at 180°C fan/200°C/gas 6 and serve with the dressing as above.

GRIDDLED PORTOBELLO MUSHROOMS & LEEKS WITH TARRAGON & WALNUTS

This is a robust dish, with big hits of flavour from the tarragon and walnuts. Serve with good bread alongside.

Serves: 4
Prep: 15 minutes
Cook: 20 minutes

4 medium leeks
600g portobello mushrooms, whole
4 tablespoons olive oil
1 teaspoon sea salt flakes

FOR THE DRESSING
3 tablespoons extra virgin olive oil
1 lemon, zest and juice
10g fresh tarragon, leaves only,
   finely chopped
50g walnuts, roughly chopped
1 teaspoon sea salt flakes

Leave the tough outer skin on the leeks, trim off the green tops, then slice them into 5cm logs. Put them into a large bowl with the mushrooms, then add the olive oil and sea salt flakes and gently mix until evenly coated.

For the dressing, stir together the olive oil, lemon zest and juice, tarragon, walnuts and sea salt flakes. Taste and adjust the salt and lemon as needed, then set aside.

Once your barbecue is good and hot, grill the leeks and mushrooms, turning them every 5 minutes, until the mushrooms are cooked through and the leeks are charred on the outside and soft within – this should take 15–20 minutes.

Discard the outer, very charred skin from the leeks if you wish. Arrange on a platter with the mushrooms, drizzle over the tarragon and walnut dressing, and serve hot.

BARBECUED CORN
WITH SAGE & PINE NUT BUTTER

This is – if I say so myself – an inspired way to dress crisp grilled corn. Crunch from the pine nuts, sage warmed through by the melting butter – a bit like your favourite ravioli dressing, albeit on a different carb. Use a plant-based spread or good olive oil for a vegan version of this dish.

Serves: 4
Prep: 10 minutes
Cook: 20 minutes

4 corn on the cob
2 tablespoons olive oil
1½ teaspoons sea salt flakes
1 tablespoon butter
1 tablespoon pine nuts, chopped
10 fresh sage leaves, finely chopped
½ clove of garlic, finely chopped

In a large bowl, evenly coat the corn with the oil and 1 teaspoon of sea salt flakes.

Mix the butter, pine nuts, sage leaves, garlic and ½ teaspoon of sea salt flakes, and set aside.

Once your barbecue is good and hot, cook the corn for 4–5 minutes on each side, turning as each side grills, until the whole cob is evenly charred to your liking.

Spread the sage and pine nut butter over the corn as soon as it comes off the barbecue, and serve hot.

Cook indoors: Roast the corn in the oven for 45 minutes at 180°C fan/200°C/gas 6 and dress with the butter as above.

OREGANO, PINE NUT & MOZZARELLA STUFFED MUSHROOMS WITH CHILLI

I love a stuffed mushroom; these supersized offerings take minutes to put together and taste like a hot summer day in the Mediterranean. To veganise, use good chopped seasoned tofu or plant-based soft cheese as an alternative to the mozzarella. Serve in buns, like burgers, or with ciabatta on the side.

Serves: 4
Prep: 10 minutes
Cook: 15 minutes

250g mozzarella, roughly chopped
10g fresh oregano, leaves only
30g pine nuts
½ fresh red chilli, finely chopped
½ lemon, zest and juice
1 teaspoon sea salt flakes
4–6 giant portobello mushrooms,
　stems removed
Olive oil, for brushing

TO SERVE
20g pine nuts, roughly chopped
5g fresh oregano, leaves only
½ fresh red chilli, finely chopped

Mix the mozzarella, oregano, pine nuts, chilli, lemon zest and juice and sea salt flakes together. Taste and adjust the salt as needed, and set aside.

Once your barbecue is good and hot, brush the mushrooms all over with olive oil and place on the barbecue, with the side you're going to fill down, and the smooth side up. Cook for 7–10 minutes, until softened, then flip them over.

Carefully fill the mushroom caps with the mozzarella mixture, packing it down gently with a spoon. (You may wish to take the mushrooms off the barbecue and put them on a plate to do this.)

Cook the mushrooms smooth side down, filling side up, for a further 7–10 minutes – if you've got particularly giant mushrooms, you can cook them lid down or by inverting a metal roasting tin or bowl over the top to create an oven effect.

Once the mushrooms are cooked through and the mozzarella has melted, arrange on a plate, scatter over the pine nuts, oregano and chilli, and serve hot.

GRIDDLED AUBERGINE
WITH CUCUMBER, WALNUTS & CUMIN

I love this dish, with the hot, blackened aubergine against the crisp, cold cucumber and the warming walnut and cumin – a refreshing combination, and perfect for a hot day. Aubergine cooked on the barbecue tastes like nothing else, but I've given options for making this dish indoors as well, so you can have it year-round.

Serves: 4 as a side
Prep: 10 minutes
Cook: 20 minutes tops

2 aubergines, cut into 1cm slices
2 teaspoons sea salt flakes
2 teaspoons cumin seeds,
   roughly ground
½ cucumber, cut into 1cm slices
2 tablespoons olive oil,
   plus more for brushing
2 tablespoons walnuts,
   roughly chopped
½ lemon, juice only

Rub the aubergine slices with half the salt and roughly ground cumin seeds. Once your barbecue is good and hot, brush the aubergine on both sides with the olive oil, and place on the barbecue grill. Cook for 4–5 minutes until well charred, then flip and repeat on the other side, until cooked through.

Meanwhile, mix the cucumber, remaining roughly ground cumin, oil, walnuts, lemon juice and sea salt together, and leave to marinate.

Once your aubergine is cooked, arrange on a platter, and scatter over the cucumber and walnut mix. Serve hot, or at room temperature.

Cook indoors: Cook the aubergine as above but in batches in a ridged griddle pan, or roast in a single layer on a large baking sheet for about 25 minutes at 200°C fan/220°C/gas 7, until well browned and cooked through.

SPICED PARMESAN CORN WITH LEMON & MINT

The secret ingredient in this spiced corn is cumin – it works so well with the Parmesan. Addictive, as all barbecued corn is.

Serves: 4–6
Prep: 10 minutes
Cook: 15 minutes

4–6 corn on the cob
2 tablespoons olive oil
¼ teaspoon cayenne pepper
1 teaspoon ground cumin
1 teaspoon sea salt flakes
40g vegetarian Parmesan,
    finely grated
A handful of fresh mint,
    finely chopped

Tip the corn, olive oil, cayenne, cumin and sea salt flakes into a large bowl and mix until the corn is completely coated in the spices and oil.

Once your barbecue is good and hot, cook the corn for 2–3 minutes on all sides, until evenly charred.

Meanwhile, tip your grated Parmesan into a roasting tin large enough to hold all four pieces of corn on the cob. As soon as the corn is cooked and off the barbecue, tip it into the tin with the cheese, and give it a good shake to evenly coat it. The cheese will start melting into the hot corn – scatter over the chopped mint, and serve with skewers to eat as soon as you can.

YUZU MUSHROOMS WITH CORIANDER & CASHEWS

You can find tiny bottles of yuzu juice along with Japanese rice vinegar and soy in larger supermarkets – it's the juice of a South East Asian citrus fruit, like a more floral and very addictive version of lime juice. Worth splashing out for this unusual side dish – you can use it instead of lime juice in other Asian style dressings.

Serves: 4
Prep: 10 minutes
Cook: 15 minutes

600g portobello mushrooms, whole
3 tablespoons sesame oil
1 teaspoon sea salt flakes
A handful of chopped fresh
   coriander
A handful of toasted chopped
   cashews

FOR THE DRESSING
3 tablespoons yuzu juice
2 tablespoons sesame oil
A pinch of sea salt flakes

Toss the mushrooms in a large bowl with the sesame oil and sea salt flakes.

For the dressing, stir the yuzu juice, sesame oil and sea salt flakes together. Taste and adjust the salt and yuzu as needed, then set aside.

Once your barbecue is good and hot, grill the mushrooms, turning them every 5 minutes, until they are cooked through – this should take 15–20 minutes.

Arrange the mushrooms on a platter, drizzle over the yuzu dressing, and scatter over the chopped coriander and cashews (eagle-eyed readers may note that there are no cashews opposite: we'd eaten half the dish before realising I'd left them in the oven. But don't let that stop you using them).

HALLOUMI STUFFED AUBERGINE
WITH LEMON & OREGANO

In this dish, thinly sliced aubergines are softened on the barbecue while you marinate sticks of halloumi in lemon, oregano and mint. When the aubergines are just soft, you roll them around the cheese, and return them to the barbecue to char: one of my favourite recipes.

Serves: 4
Prep: 15 minutes
Cook: under 15 minutes

2 fat aubergines
Olive oil, for brushing
250g halloumi,
    cut into 1½ cm
    rectangular sticks
2 tablespoons fresh mint leaves,
    roughly chopped
2 tablespoons fresh oregano
    leaves, roughly chopped
1 lemon, juice only
Cocktail sticks
2 tablespoons extra virgin olive oil

Cut each aubergine into 8 thin slices, then brush the slices on one side with olive oil. Once your barbecue is hot (you can pop these on as the barbecue is just getting warm, too), put the aubergine slices on, oil side down, and brush the tops with a little more oil. Let them just soften through without colouring, then flip them over and repeat on the other side.

Meanwhile, mix your halloumi sticks, mint, oregano and lemon juice together, and set aside. Once your aubergine slices are softened and cool enough to handle, wrap each piece of halloumi in a slice of aubergine, and secure with a cocktail stick. Keep the bowl of marinade for later.

Transfer to the barbecue and griddle for 2–3 minutes on each side, until the aubergine is nicely charred and cooked through.

Add the extra virgin olive oil to the bowl containing the remaining herb and lemon juice marinade. Once the stuffed aubergines are ready, transfer them to a serving platter and pour the lemon and herb dressing over the top. Serve hot.

Note: If you want to prepare these ahead, you can soften the aubergine slices in a roasting tin in a hot oven first, being careful not to let them colour. Follow the instructions up to the end of step 2, then cool and refrigerate them until you're ready to barbecue, or finish on a hot griddle pan.

CAULIFLOWER & CABBAGE

Technically brassicas, but who calls them that?
A lovely textural contrast for your barbecue.

**SPICED BUTTER CAULIFLOWER
WITH MARINATED FETA & LEMON**

**SMOKED RED CABBAGE WITH APPLES,
RAISINS & PECANS**

**CRISPY GINGER CAULIFLOWER WINGS
WITH TAMARIND & CORIANDER (VEGAN)**

**BARBECUED SPROUTS WITH CHILLI,
LEMON & ALMONDS (VEGAN)**

**CRISPY CABBAGE
WITH CHILLI SAGE BREADCRUMBS (VEGAN)**

SPICED BUTTER CAULIFLOWER
WITH MARINATED FETA & LEMON

While I enjoy the restrained drama of a whole cauliflower, carved at the table, you can reduce the time between prep and consumption by cutting your cauliflower into large steaks. This version with spiced butter and marinated feta is a favourite.

Serves: 4
Prep: 15 minutes
Cook: 25 minutes

1 large cauliflower, plus its leaves
8 cardamom pods, seeds only
2 teaspoons coriander seeds
2 tablespoons melted butter
1 teaspoon sea salt flakes
1 teaspoon chilli flakes
1 tablespoon olive oil

FOR THE MARINATED FETA
200g feta, cut into small pieces
3 tablespoons extra virgin olive oil
½ lemon, juice only
3 pieces of lemon peel
A pinch of chilli flakes
1 teaspoon coriander seeds,
  crushed
A handful of fresh mint leaves,
  roughly chopped

Trim the base of the cauliflower, then carefully slice it into 2½ cm 'steaks' – you should have at least 4. (Save the trimmings, and roast them with a little oil, sea salt and smoked paprika to have as a snack.)

Bash the cardamom and coriander seeds in a pestle and mortar, then mix with the melted butter, sea salt flakes and chilli flakes. Brush the mixture all over the cauliflower steaks, toss the cauliflower leaves with the olive oil, and set both aside.

Gently stir the feta with the olive oil, lemon juice, lemon peel, chilli flakes, coriander seeds and mint, and set aside.

Once your barbecue is good and hot, grill the cauliflower steaks for 10 minutes on one side, and 5–8 minutes on the other side, until nicely charred and just cooked through. When your cauliflower has about 10 minutes left, grill the reserved leaves for 2–3 minutes, or until crisp.

Arrange the steaks and leaves on a platter and scatter over the marinated feta and dressing. Serve hot.

SMOKED RED CABBAGE WITH APPLES, RAISINS & PECANS

You'll get maximum flavour in this dish using a charcoal barbecue and a good handful of dry twigs – I like to use apple or plum. The smoke infuses into the cabbage, and makes a filling salad.

Serves: 4
Prep: 15 minutes
Cook: 20 minutes

1 red cabbage,
    cut into eighths,
    leaves separated
2 tablespoons olive oil
1 teaspoon sea salt flakes
1 Pink Lady apple, cored
    and cut into eighths
100g raisins
100g pecans

FOR THE DRESSING
10g fresh chives, finely chopped
150ml sour cream or yogurt
½ lemon, juice only
A pinch of sea salt flakes

Toss the cabbage leaves, olive oil and sea salt flakes in a large bowl until the leaves are evenly coated. Once your barbecue is good and hot, grill the leaves for 3–4 minutes on each side, until cooked through – you can let them crisp up and char, or take them off just before they start to catch.

Meanwhile, mix together the chives, sour cream or yogurt, lemon juice and sea salt flakes, tasting and adjusting the seasoning as needed.

Pile the cooked and charred leaves onto a large platter, scatter over the apples, raisins and pecans, and serve warm, with the sour cream dressing.

Note: If you prefer, you can let the cooked leaves cool a little, then roll them up and shred them – easier to spoon up just with a fork.

CRISPY GINGER CAULIFLOWER WINGS WITH TAMARIND & CORIANDER

These cauliflower wings are ridiculously moreish, and the sauce – made with bought jarred tamarind – couldn't be easier. Double up the quantities for a crowd.

Serves: 4 as a snack
Prep: 10 minutes
Cook: 10 minutes

1 large cauliflower,
  cut into small florets,
  plus its leaves
2 tablespoons olive or neutral oil
2 teaspoons ground ginger,
  or grated fresh ginger
1 teaspoon sea salt flakes
A handful of fresh coriander,
chopped

FOR THE DRESSING
30g tamarind paste, from a jar
  (not tamarind concentrate)
15ml olive oil

Tip the cauliflower florets and leaves into a large bowl along with the oil, ginger and sea salt flakes. Mix well until everything is evenly coated.

Once your barbecue is good and hot, cook the florets for 3–4 minutes each side until charred and cooked through: the leaves will take about 2 minutes per side.

In the bowl you used for the cauliflower, mix the tamarind paste and the olive oil to make the dressing. Taste and add salt if needed – most supermarket tamarind paste is salted, so you probably won't need any. As soon as the cauliflower florets and leaves are cooked, tip them into the bowl with the dressing, and toss to coat.

Tip the cauliflower onto a serving dish, scatter over the chopped coriander, and serve hot.

BARBECUED SPROUTS WITH CHILLI, LEMON & ALMONDS

Sprouts on a barbecue? They remind me very much of chestnuts, and to my mind only benefit from a quick blast on the coals. Dressed with punchy chilli and lemon, these are an exceptional side.

Serves: 4 as a side
Prep: 10 minutes
Cook: 10 minutes tops

200g large Brussels sprouts, halved
   (leave the small ones whole)
2 tablespoons olive oil
1 teaspoon sea salt flakes
50g flaked almonds, toasted
A handful of fresh flat-leaf parsley,
   roughly chopped

FOR THE DRESSING
1 fresh red chilli, finely chopped
1 lemon, zest and juice
2 tablespoons extra virgin olive oil
1 teaspoon sea salt flakes

Mix the halved and whole sprouts with the olive oil and sea salt flakes in a large bowl.

Stir the chilli, lemon zest and juice, olive oil and sea salt together, taste and adjust the salt and lemon as needed, and set aside.

Once your barbecue is at a medium heat, cook the sprouts for 5–6 minutes on each side, until charred and just cooked through.

Dress the cooked sprouts with the lemon and chilli dressing, and serve scattered with the flaked almonds and flat-leaf parsley.

CRISPY CABBAGE
WITH CHILLI SAGE BREADCRUMBS

One of my favourite dishes in the book – cabbage is just glorious on the barbecue, crispy at the edges, gently steamed inside. With chilli and sage through the crispy breadcrumbs, these are exceptional.

Serves: 4
Prep: 15 minutes
Cook: 15 minutes tops

1 sweetheart cabbage
2 tablespoons olive oil
1 teaspoon sea salt flakes

FOR THE SAGE CRUMBS
3 tablespoons olive oil
10 fresh sage leaves, finely chopped
½ teaspoon chipotle chilli flakes
A pinch of sea salt flakes
50g panko or white breadcrumbs
½ large lemon, juice only, to serve

Cut the cabbage into eighths, leaving the stem intact so the pieces stay together. Gently dress with the olive oil and sea salt, rubbing as much as possible into the cut surfaces and leaves.

Heat the oil in a frying pan on a medium heat, and add the sage leaves, chilli flakes and sea salt. Fry for 2–3 minutes, until the sage starts to colour, then add the breadcrumbs. Lower the heat and stir occasionally for 5–6 minutes, until the crumbs are evenly golden brown. Let the breadcrumbs cool (easy to forget), then taste and add salt as needed.

Once your barbecue is medium to hot, grill the cabbage for 6–8 minutes per side, until just charred and cooked through. (If you stick a fork into the cabbage, it should yield easily.)

Pile the cabbage onto a platter, dress with the lemon juice, scatter over the sage crumbs, and serve hot.

Note: Keep any leftover crumbs to scatter over hot pasta or a gratin.

HOW TO MAKE A SALAD

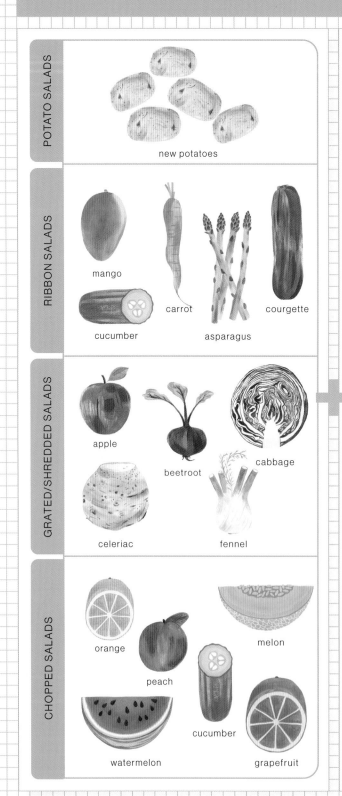

POTATO SALADS

new potatoes

RIBBON SALADS

mango

carrot

asparagus

courgette

cucumber

GRATED/SHREDDED SALADS

apple

beetroot

cabbage

celeriac

fennel

CHOPPED SALADS

orange

peach

melon

watermelon

cucumber

grapefruit

SOMETHING SHARP

red onion

chives

spring onion

SOMETHING GREEN

rocket

lamb's lettuce

pea shoots

watercress

SOMETHING HERBY

coriander

basil

tarragon

parsley

dill

mint

THE ALL-IMPORTANT DRESSING BASE

OLIVE & LEMON DRESSING

 1 tablespoon extra virgin olive oil

 1 lemon, juice only

 ½ teaspoon sea salt flakes

SESAME & LIME DRESSING

 1 tablespoon sesame oil

 1 lime, juice only

 ½ teaspoon sea salt flakes

VINEGAR DRESSING

 1 tablespoon extra virgin olive oil

 1 tablespoon red or white wine vinegar

 ½ teaspoon sea salt flakes

SESAME SOY DRESSING

 1 tablespoon sesame oil

 1 tablespoon rice wine vinegar

 1 tablespoon soy sauce

SOMETHING HOT

harissa

Dijon mustard

ground black pepper

chilli

PERHAPS DAIRY

yogurt

mayonnaise

SOMETHING CRUNCHY

peanuts

walnuts

almonds

pecans

hazelnuts

AND MAYBE CHEESE

feta

goat's cheese

blue cheese

mozzarella

POTATO SALADS

750G WAXY/NEW POTATOES
(ANYA, CHARLOTTE,
JERSEY ROYALS ETC.)

Boil in salted water until tender, halve,
then combine as shown on pages 148-149

RIBBON SALADS

A COMBINATION OF YOUR CHOICE
OF MANGO, CARROT, CUCUMBER,
ASPARAGUS OR COURGETTE

Slice into ribbons using a speed peeler,
then combine as shown on pages 148-149

GRATED/SHREDDED SALADS

A COMBINATION OF YOUR CHOICE
OF FENNEL, BEETROOT, APPLES,
CELERIAC OR CABBAGE

Grate using a box grater, grating attachment of
your food processor, or thinly slice,
then combine as shown on pages 148-149

CHOPPED SALADS

A COMBINATION OF YOUR CHOICE
OF CUCUMBER, PEACH, MELON,
GRAPEFRUIT, ORANGE OR WATERMELON

Chop or slice into large chunks,
then combine as as shown on pages 148-149

THREE WAYS WITH AVOCADO

MANGO & AVOCADO SALSA

1 avocado, just underripe,
chopped into ½ cm cubes

1 mango, just underripe,
chopped into ½ cm cubes

½ pomegranate,
seeds only

1 fresh red chilli,
finely chopped

2 limes, zest
and juice

20g fresh basil   sea salt flakes,
leaves, torn   to taste

Serves: 4 generously
Prep time: 15 minutes

Mix everything together, then
taste and adjust the salt.
Serve at room temperature –
you can make this a few hours
ahead and chill until needed.

TOMATO & RED ONION GUACAMOLE

3 ripe avocados

½ red onion,
very finely chopped

1 small tomato,
finely chopped

20g fresh coriander,
finely chopped

2 teaspoons   2 limes,
sea salt flakes juice only

Serves: 6 generously
Prep time: 15 minutes

Roughly chop or mash the
avocado flesh, then mix
with the onion, tomato and
coriander. Add lime juice and
sea salt flakes to taste.

GRAPEFRUIT, AVOCADO & PINEAPPLE SALSA

1 avocado, just underripe,
cut into 1cm cubes

1 grapefruit,
cut into 1cm cubes

½ fresh pineapple,
cut into ½ cm cubes

20g fresh mint,   2 limes,
finely chopped   juice only

1 teaspoon
sea salt flakes

Serves: 6 generously
Prep time: 15 minutes

Mix the avocado, grapefruit,
pineapple, mint, lime juice and
sea salt flakes together just
before you're ready to eat.
Adjust the salt and serve.

THREE WAYS WITH SOUR CREAM

Serves: 4
Prep: 10 minutes

300ml sour cream
or natural yogurt

Stir the sour cream or yogurt in a bowl with your chosen variation ingredients, then taste and adjust the salt as needed. Serve at room temperature – you can make these a few hours ahead and chill before bringing them out as needed.

ROASTED GARLIC TZATZIKI

3 cloves of garlic

¼ cucumber,
seeds removed, grated

½ tablespoon
olive oil

sea salt flakes,
to taste

Roast the garlic with the olive oil for 20 minutes at 180°C fan/200°C/gas 6 (ideally alongside another dish in the oven so you aren't turning it on just for the garlic – I often make an entire trayful from 2 or 3 bulbs of garlic with a generous amount of olive oil, then peel and store them in the fridge for future use).

Squeeze out the roasted garlic and mix it with the sour cream and grated cucumber. Add sea salt flakes to taste, and serve.

SPRING ONION & LIME

6 spring onions,
finely chopped

1 lime,
zest and juice

sea salt flakes, to taste

BLUE CHEESE & CHIVE

100g blue cheese,
crumbled

10g chives,
finely chopped

sea salt flakes, to taste

THREE WAYS WITH BURNT AUBERGINE

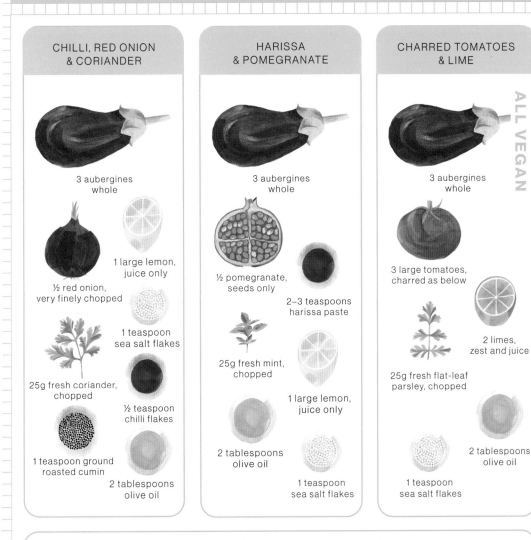

CHILLI, RED ONION & CORIANDER

3 aubergines whole

½ red onion, very finely chopped

1 large lemon, juice only

1 teaspoon sea salt flakes

25g fresh coriander, chopped

½ teaspoon chilli flakes

1 teaspoon ground roasted cumin

2 tablespoons olive oil

HARISSA & POMEGRANATE

3 aubergines whole

½ pomegranate, seeds only

2–3 teaspoons harissa paste

25g fresh mint, chopped

1 large lemon, juice only

2 tablespoons olive oil

1 teaspoon sea salt flakes

CHARRED TOMATOES & LIME

3 aubergines whole

3 large tomatoes, charred as below

2 limes, zest and juice

25g fresh flat-leaf parsley, chopped

2 tablespoons olive oil

1 teaspoon sea salt flakes

ALL VEGAN

Serves: 4
Prep: 15 minutes
Cook: 30–40 minutes

Place the aubergines directly on the hot coals of your barbecue, and turn them after about 20 minutes. You want the skin to completely blacken, and when you insert a knife, the insides should feel soft, as if the aubergine has collapsed from the inside. Alternatively, you can do this under a scorchingly hot grill for 15 minutes on each side. Let the burnt aubergines cool down a bit, and once you're able to handle them, halve and scoop out the flesh.

Mash the flesh in a bowl with your chosen variation ingredients. Think of this like making a pesto – you're adding salt, oil and lemon or lime juice to taste, so follow the recipe, then taste and adjust until you are happy with the flavour.

If you are making the variation with charred tomatoes, brush the whole tomatoes with oil, and place on a hot barbecue to grill for 7–8 minutes on each side. You can do the same indoors under a very hot grill.

NAAN

GARLIC, CORIANDER & CUMIN

2 cloves of garlic, grated or crushed

1 tablespoon coriander seeds, crushed

1 tablespoon cumin seeds, crushed

BEETROOT & CUMIN

100g grated beetroot

1 tablespoon cumin seeds, crushed

POMEGRANATE & CORIANDER

3 tablespoons pomegranate seeds

3 tablespoons chopped fresh coriander

1 tablespoon nigella seeds

Makes:	4 naan breads	300g plain flour
Prep:	15 minutes,	1 teaspoon baking powder
	plus 1 hour resting	1 teaspoon sea salt flakes
Cook:	3 minutes	1 teaspoon sugar
		1 tablespoon melted butter
		(or ghee), plus extra for brushing
		200ml milk

Mix together the flour, baking powder, sea salt flakes, sugar and butter, and gradually work in the milk until you have a stiff dough, adding in your variation ingredients as detailed above. Knead for 5–10 minutes. Cover in an oiled bowl, then leave to rest for 1–2 hours.

Once your barbecue is good and hot, divide the dough into 4 equal pieces. Roll the dough out into circles about the size of a large saucer, then pull each into a teardrop shape. Leave them to rest for 5 minutes.

Oil the barbecue grill, then cook the bread for about 1–1½ minutes on each side, until blackened in spots and cooked through. Brush with more butter and serve warm.

Cook indoors: Heat your grill to a medium-high setting and preheat a heavy baking sheet. Arrange the pieces on the hot baking sheet and grill for 2–3 minutes, until cooked through.

FLATBREAD

FIG, FETA & FENNEL

2 fresh figs,
chopped

100g feta cheese, crumbled

2 teaspoons
fennel seeds

WALNUT & HERB

60g walnuts,
finely chopped

40g finely chopped
soft fresh herbs
(coriander, parsley etc.)

PEAR, RICOTTA & HONEY

2 small firm pears,
grated

6 tablespoons   6 teaspoons
ricotta   honey

A pinch of freshly ground
black pepper

Serves: 4–6
Prep: 5–10 minutes, plus 1 hour resting
Cook: 2–4 minutes

75ml olive oil
1 teaspoon sea salt flakes
200ml warm water
1 teaspoon honey
400g strong white bread flour
1 teaspoon fast-action dried yeast

Mix all the base dough ingredients together and knead for 5–10 minutes, until smooth. Transfer the dough to an oiled bowl, cover, and leave to rise for 1 hour or until doubled in size.

Punch down the dough, then for variations one and two, knead through your chosen flavourings, using a little flour if the dough becomes too sticky. Divide the dough into 6 and roll out into 20cm rounds.

Brush your barbecue with oil, and cook the flatbreads on a medium-hot grill for 2–4 minutes per side, until just cooked through and charred. Serve hot.

For the pear and ricotta flatbreads, squeeze the excess water from the grated pear. Divide the dough into 6, and on a floured surface, roll each piece into a circle the size of a side plate.

Scatter a tablespoon of ricotta and pear in the centre, leaving a 4cm border around the edges, and drizzle with a teaspoon of honey and a little freshly ground black pepper. Fold three sides of your dough in, and gently pat down into a triangle, rolling very gently to enclose the filling.

Cook indoors: You can bake these in the oven for 8–10 minutes at 210°C fan/230°C/gas 8.

TAKE IT TO THE BEACH (OR PARK)

PORTABLE BARBECUE FOOD – JUST PACK,
AND STICK IT ON A SMALL BARBECUE
WHEN YOU GET THERE.

TAKE IT TO THE BEACH (OR PARK)

———————

**AUBERGINE & GOAT'S CHEESE BURGER STACKS
WITH HONEY & THYME**

RED PEPPER, FETA, BASIL & PINE NUT PARCELS

**SIMPLE SAGE & ONION CANNELLINI BURGERS
(VEGAN)**

**CHIPOTLE MUSHROOM & BLACK BEAN BURGERS
WITH PEANUTS & LIME (VEGAN)**

LEEK & CHEDDAR GLAMORGAN SAUSAGES

**SICHUAN AUBERGINE WEDGES
WITH BLACK BEAN SAUCE (VEGAN)**

**LIME PICKLE, BUTTERNUT SQUASH
& HALLOUMI BURGERS**

TANDOORI FENNEL STEAKS WITH MINT RAITA

**LIME & CHILLI SWEETCORN FRITTERS
WITH ROASTED TOMATOES**

**CHILLI CHEESE FRENCH-TOASTED CRUMPETS
WITH SAGE**

**SECRET GARDEN WHOLE ROASTED EGGS
& NEW POTATOES WITH SALSA VERDE**

AUBERGINE & GOAT'S CHEESE BURGER STACKS WITH HONEY & THYME

One of my favourite Spanish dishes is *berenjenas con miel* – aubergines, deep-fried in batter, served with honey. It occurred to me that goat's cheese is just as lovely with honey as aubergine, and so these moreish burger stacks were born. The cheese melts between the aubergine slices, scented with thyme – perfect by themselves or squashed between crusty white rolls.

Serves: 4
Prep: 10 minutes
Cook: 30 minutes

2 large, evenly sized aubergines
2 x 100g rind-on goat's cheese
   wheels
A handful of fresh lemon thyme
   sprigs
Olive oil, for brushing
Sea salt flakes
Freshly ground black pepper
Runny honey
Crusty bread rolls, to serve

Cut the aubergines into 1cm slices, and the goat's cheese into very thin rounds. Sandwich each piece of goat's cheese between two similarly sized slices of aubergine, along with a sprig of thyme. Brush both sides of the aubergine with oil and add a tiny pinch of sea salt flakes and black pepper.

Once your barbecue is ready, place the aubergine stacks on the grill and cook for 10–15 minutes per side, until the aubergine is cooked through and the cheese has melted. You can flip them every 5–6 minutes or so and give them a brush with olive oil.

Transfer to a serving platter, drizzle with honey, scatter over the remaining thyme, and serve with crusty rolls on the side.

RED PEPPER, FETA, BASIL & PINE NUT PARCELS

In this recipe, I use the cut halves of red peppers to hold the filling, so what you get is somewhere between a supersized stuffed pepper and a squashable, melted-cheese-filled burger. It reminds me of a scene in *The Godfather,* where a mobster fries up red peppers to make a simple, but delicious sandwich.

Serves: 4
Prep: 15 minutes
Cook: 30 minutes

4 red peppers, halved
  and deseeded
50g pine nuts
200g feta cheese, crumbled
1 lemon, zest and juice
A handful of fresh basil, chopped
1 fresh red chilli, chopped

Brush both sides of the halved peppers with a little olive oil. Once your barbecue is medium hot, barbecue the peppers for about 10 minutes on each side, until charred and slightly softened.

Remove the softened peppers, and stuff 4 of the halves with the feta and basil mixture. Lay the other 4 pepper halves on top, and return them to the barbecue for a further 5 minutes on each side to warm the feta through.

Eat as they are, or stuffed into burger buns.

SIMPLE SAGE & ONION CANNELLINI BURGERS

I used to use this combination as a filling for vegan sausage rolls, and with a little experimentation came up with this version in burger form – perfect in rolls with a spoon of mustard on the side.

Serves: 6
Prep: 20 minutes
Cook: 30 minutes

200g small potatoes, whole
1 large white onion, roughly chopped
2 cloves garlic, whole
1 teaspoon freshly ground
   black pepper
1 teaspoon sea salt flakes
10 sage leaves, roughly chopped
1 tablespoon olive oil
1 x 400g of tin cannellini beans,
   drained well, but not rinsed
2 teaspoons Dijon mustard
2 teaspoons cornflour
6 burger buns, to serve

Tip the potatoes, onion, garlic, pepper, salt, sage and olive oil into a small roasting tin. Roast for 30 minutes at 180°C fan/200°C/gas 6 until the potatoes are cooked through and the onions soft.

Squeeze the garlic out from their skins, then pulse the vegetables together with the cannellini beans, mustard and cornflour in the food processor – you want the texture of a thick mash.

Taste the mixture and add salt as needed, then use tablespoons to form into six burger patties on a lined baking sheet.

Bake the burgers at 180°C fan/200°C/gas 6 for 25–30 minutes, until golden brown and crisp. You can eat them immediately at this stage, or if packing them for a picnic, let them cool down, then give them a final blast for a couple of minutes per side on a hot, well-oiled barbecue.

CHIPOTLE MUSHROOM & BLACK BEAN BURGERS WITH PEANUTS & LIME

These burgers are ridiculously moreish – I like to serve them in buns with mayonnaise and pickles. Make life easier for yourself by cooking them in the oven first, then finishing them off with a quick warm-through on the barbecue before serving.

Serves: 4
Prep: 20 minutes
Cook: 25 minutes

50g smooth peanut butter
1 x 400g tin of black beans,
   drained, but not rinsed
2 small cloves of garlic, peeled
2 teaspoons chipotle chilli flakes
1 teaspoon ground cumin
1 tablespoon olive oil
1 heaped tablespoon rye flour
1 lime, zest only
1 teaspoon sea salt flakes
250g chestnut mushrooms

TO SERVE
1 lime, cut into 4 wedges
A handful of chopped salted
   peanuts
A handful of chopped fresh
   coriander
4 burger buns

Put the peanut butter into a food processor with 60g of the black beans, the garlic, chilli flakes, cumin, olive oil, rye flour, lime zest and sea salt flakes, and blitz until you have a very thick paste. Tip it into a large bowl and stir in the rest of the black beans.

Tip the mushrooms into the processor – no need to wash it – and pulse until you have a dry mushroom mince. Stir this into the black bean mixture. With damp hands, form it into four thick burgers and arrange them on a lined baking sheet.

Bake in the oven at 180°C fan/200°C/gas 6 for 25–30 minutes. When they've got 10 minutes left, gently flip them over so they can crisp up on the other side.

They're ready to serve straight from the oven, but for a nice bit of smokiness you can let them cool down, then finish them on a medium barbecue for a couple of minutes per side.

Squeeze over the lime wedges and top with a handful of chopped peanuts and coriander, then sandwich them into lightly grilled burger buns.

LEEK & CHEDDAR GLAMORGAN SAUSAGES

These are inspired by the classic Welsh Glamorgan sausages, adapted for the barbecue with three of my favourite ingredients – cheddar, mustard and sage. You can part-bake these in advance in the oven, and finish them off on the barbecue – perfect to transport to the park or beach.

Serves: 4 generously
Prep: 30 minutes, plus 1 hour chilling
Cook: 30 minutes

2 tablespoons olive oil
2 leeks, thinly sliced
1 teaspoon sea salt flakes
150g cheddar, grated
1 heaped teaspoon mustard
10 sage leaves, finely chopped
2 free-range egg yolks
100g fresh white breadcrumbs
1 teaspoon freshly ground
　black pepper
Plain flour, for shaping
4 hot-dog rolls and mustard,
　for serving

Heat the oil in a medium saucepan, add the leeks and sea salt flakes, then stir, cover and soften for 10 minutes on a low heat, stirring occasionally. Once the leeks have softened, let them cool down, then press them between a few sheets of kitchen roll to remove any excess moisture.

Mix the leeks with the grated cheese, mustard, sage, egg yolks, breadcrumbs and black pepper. With lightly floured hands, form the mixture into 8 small sausages and put them on a floured plate. Cover and chill for at least an hour, or overnight.

Preheat the oven to 180°C fan/200°C/gas 6. Transfer the sausages to a lined baking sheet, brush them with olive oil, and bake for 30 minutes. Then finish them off on the barbecue for a few minutes on each side to char.

Serve in hot-dog rolls, 2 to each roll, with more mustard.

SICHUAN AUBERGINE WEDGES WITH BLACK BEAN SAUCE

Aubergines cooked with black bean sauce are ridiculously moreish – serve them alongside a range of other South East Asian-inspired dishes (see pages 60, 98 & 100) for a themed barbecue.

Serves: 4
Prep: 15 minutes
Cook: 15 minutes

3 tablespoons black bean sauce
1 tablespoon sesame oil
2 aubergines, cut into 2cm slices

FOR THE DRESSING
2 tablespoons sesame oil
1 tablespoon rice vinegar
4 spring onions, thinly sliced
1 fresh red chilli, thinly sliced
1 clove of garlic, finely chopped
    or grated
5cm fresh ginger, finely chopped
    or grated
1 teaspoon caster sugar

Mix the black bean sauce with the sesame oil in a large bowl, then gently stir through the aubergine slices until evenly coated.

Once your barbecue is good and hot, cook the aubergine slices for 6–7 minutes per side, until lightly charred and cooked through.

For the dressing, mix the sesame oil, vinegar, spring onions, chilli, garlic, ginger and sugar. (The black bean sauce has a lot of salt in, so there's no extra salt in the dressing.)

Once the aubergines are done, arrange them on a platter and pour over the dressing. Taste and adjust the seasoning if needed, and serve hot.

LIME PICKLE, BUTTERNUT SQUASH & HALLOUMI BURGERS

This is a wonderful flavour combination, with sweetness from the squash, depth from the halloumi and a secret ingredient – lime pickle, inspired by Laura Goodman's cheese straws in her fantastic cookbook *Carbs*. These are perfect to part-cook in the oven, then crisp up on the barbecue.

Serves: 6
Prep: 20 minutes
Cook: 30 minutes

450g squash
125g halloumi, grated
75g lime pickle, roughly chopped
1 free-range egg, beaten
30g panko breadcrumbs
Olive oil, for brushing

TO SERVE
Yogurt
Toasted burger buns

Preheat the oven to 180°C fan/200°C/gas 6. Peel, deseed and grate your squash – you should be left with 350g. Place in a clean tea towel, then twist into a tight ball and squeeze out as much liquid as you can. Mix it well with the grated halloumi, lime pickle, egg and breadcrumbs, then form into 6 patties and put them on a lined baking tray. If you have time, put the baking tray into the fridge and chill for 30 minutes to an hour before cooking.

Transfer to the oven and bake for 20 minutes. At this point, you can take them out, let them cool down, pack and refrigerate them, then finish them off on a hot barbecue (make sure to oil the barbecue grill before) for 2–3 minutes each side, until slightly charred and warmed through.

Serve with a dollop of yogurt, and toasted burger buns.

TANDOORI FENNEL STEAKS WITH MINT RAITA

Fennel – cut into thick steaks – benefits from a longer cook over a low heat: it concentrates the sweetness. I like to make something that requires a quick flash grill on a high heat first (like the spiced Parmesan corn on page 128), and then add these once the coals have cooled to medium.

Serves: 4
Prep: 15 minutes
Cook: 20 minutes

2 round bulbs of fennel
1 teaspoon ground coriander
1 teaspoon ground cumin
1 teaspoon smoked paprika
½ teaspoon ground turmeric
½ teaspoon chilli powder
1 teaspoon sea salt flakes
2 tablespoons olive oil

FOR THE RAITA
4 tablespoons natural yogurt
¼ cucumber, seeds removed,
  grated
½ small clove of garlic, grated
1 teaspoon ground cumin
A pinch of sea salt flakes

TO SERVE
A handful of fresh mint leaves,
  roughly chopped
Flatbreads

Slice the fennel lengthways into 1½ cm steaks, leaving the stem intact to help hold them together. Mix the spices, sea salt flakes and oil in a bowl, then gently turn the fennel steaks in the spice mix until evenly coated.

Mix the yogurt, cucumber, garlic, cumin and sea salt flakes together for the raita. Taste and adjust the salt as needed, and set aside.

Once your barbecue is at a medium heat, cook the fennel steaks for 8–10 minutes on each side, until lightly charred and soft all the way through. (You can cover with a lid or an inverted roasting tin if you wish.)

Scatter the fennel steaks with the fresh mint, and serve with the raita and flatbreads alongside.

LIME & CHILLI SWEETCORN FRITTERS
WITH ROASTED TOMATOES

This is a version of a dish created originally for this book, adapted for BBC Food with tinned sweetcorn during Lockdown 2020, and adapted back again with whole sweetcorn – too nice not to include.

Serves: 4
Prep: 15 minutes
Cook: 30 minutes

4 corn on the cob
3 spring onions, thinly sliced
75g plain flour
1 teaspoon ground cumin
1 teaspoon ground coriander
1 teaspoon smoked paprika
1 teaspoon sea salt flakes
1 fresh red chilli, finely chopped
100g natural yogurt
1 free-range egg, beaten
2 limes, zest and juice

FOR THE ROASTED TOMATOES
300g cherry tomatoes, on the vine
1 tablespoon olive oil
1 teaspoon sea salt flakes

Stand the corn upright on a chopping board, and using a sharp knife, slice the kernels off each side.

Put the kernels into a large bowl with the spring onions, flour, spices, sea salt flakes and chilli, then add the yogurt, egg and the zest and juice of 1 lime, and stir until you have a thick batter.

Put the cherry tomatoes with their vines, oil and sea salt into the middle of a piece of foil the size of a chopping board and fold it together into a neat parcel, with the seams at the top.

Remove the tomatoes from the foil, discard the liquid, and mash the tomatoes into a thick sauce. Taste and adjust the salt as needed.

To start in the oven, and finish on the barbecue: Drop heaped tablespoons of batter onto a lined baking sheet and flatten. Bake at 180°C fan/200°C/gas 6 for 20 minutes, then finish the fritters on the barbecue, grilling them until crisp and golden brown.

Serve the fritters hot, with the remaining lime juice and zest, and the roasted tomato sauce alongside.

CHILLI CHEESE FRENCH-TOASTED CRUMPETS WITH SAGE

I love French toast, and I love crumpets, and this version with sage, cheddar and chilli is an indulgent snack. Serve for brunch late-morning, or as an afternoon snack.

Serves: 3–6
Prep: 10 minutes
Cook: 10 minutes

3 medium free-range eggs,
   lightly beaten
3 tablespoons yogurt
100g cheddar, grated
1 fresh red chilli, finely chopped
20 fresh sage leaves, chopped
½ teaspoon sea salt flakes
6 crumpets
Freshly ground black pepper,
   to serve

Whisk the eggs, yogurt, cheddar, chilli, sage and sea salt flakes together in a large bowl. Gently stir through your crumpets to thoroughly coat them in the mixture, letting them soak for 5–10 minutes if you have time.

When your barbecue is good and hot, fish the crumpets out of the bowl and place them on the well-oiled grill, bubbly side up. Spoon over any remaining cheese and egg mixture, grill for 3–4 minutes, then flip over and cook for a further 2–3 minutes until the egg has just set. Serve immediately, with freshly ground black pepper.

Note: For a portable version, pack your egg mixture and crumpets separately, then dip them into the mixture and barbecue them to order. You can of course also cook these in a frying pan.

SECRET GARDEN WHOLE ROASTED EGGS & NEW POTATOES WITH SALSA VERDE

I loved *The Secret Garden* growing up, and particularly when the children start experimenting with outdoor cooking to avoid suspicion at dinnertime, as their appetites have trebled thanks to their illicit gardening. I may have misremembered, but at one point I'm certain they cook eggs and potatoes whole on the embers of a fire outside. This dish, with a vibrant green salsa verde on the side, is my homage.

Serves: 4
Prep: 15 minutes
Cook: 30 minutes

600g new potatoes
2 tablespoons olive oil
1 teaspoon sea salt flakes
4 free-range eggs, whole

FOR THE SALSA VERDE
25g fresh flat-leaf parsley,
   finely chopped
A handful of fresh coriander leaves,
   finely chopped
½ clove of garlic, grated
3 tablespoons extra virgin olive oil
1 tablespoon red wine vinegar
1 teaspoon Dijon mustard
A pinch of sea salt flakes

Boil the new potatoes for 7–8 minutes, until just cooked through. Drain well, then stir through the olive oil and sea salt flakes.

For the salsa verde, stir the parsley, coriander, garlic, olive oil, vinegar, Dijon and sea salt flakes together. Taste and adjust the vinegar and salt as needed, and set aside.

Once your barbecue is medium hot, place the potatoes and the eggs on it, putting the eggs on the cooler side of the barbecue (see page 11). Grill everything for 10 minutes per side, until the potatoes are nicely golden brown and charred. You'll want to turn the eggs every 5 minutes so they cook evenly – this should take 20–25 minutes.

Dip the eggs in cold water, peel and halve them, then pile them on a plate with the crisp potatoes. Serve hot, with the salsa verde alongside.

SOMETHING SWEET

FINISH YOUR OUTDOOR FEAST WITH FRESH GRIDDLED FRUIT WITH INDULGENT MELTED CHOCOLATE, CARAMEL OR PEANUT BUTTER (OR ALL THREE).

SOMETHING SWEET

SIMPLY ROASTED APRICOTS
WITH ROSE & PISTACHIO (VEGAN)

SAFFRON PEARS & RHUBARB WITH RICOTTA

THE ELVIS AFTERNOON BARBECUE SANDWICH:
CHOCOLATE, PEANUT BUTTER & BANANA (VEGAN)

SUMMER PUDDING PACKETS:
VANILLA ROASTED BERRIES WITH TOASTED BRIOCHE,
MASCARPONE & ALMONDS

DULCE DE LECHE PASSIONFRUIT POTS
WITH CHOCOLATE & RICOTTA

ORANGE FLOWER WATER PEACHES
WITH ROSEMARY, ALMONDS & CREAM

CINNAMON GRIDDLED PINEAPPLE
WITH TOASTED COCONUT (VEGAN)

HONEY & ORANGE GRIDDLED PAPAYA
WITH MINT

SIMPLY ROASTED APRICOTS
WITH ROSE & PISTACHIO

When you've had your fill of ripe apricots (which may take some time – every time I looked for them in the kitchen to make this dish, one or two had mysteriously disappeared from the fruit bowl), try them simply griddled on the barbecue, with a lovely orange and rose dressing.

Serves: 4
Prep: 10 minutes
Cook: 10 minutes

8 just ripe apricots, halved
  and stones removed
Olive oil, for brushing
30g pistachios, roughly chopped
2 tablespoons dried rose petals
  (optional)
Demerara sugar, to serve

FOR THE DRESSING
1-2 drops of rosewater
½ orange, zest and juice
2 teaspoons caster sugar

Brush the cut side of the apricots with a little olive oil.

For the dressing, mix the rosewater with the orange zest and juice and caster sugar, stirring until the sugar has dissolved. Go very gently with the rosewater – it varies in strength, and you want to use it drop by drop until you've reached the optimum level of rosiness, as Nigella says.

Once your barbecue is at a medium heat, barbecue the apricots cut side down for about 5 minutes, or until just starting to char.

Tumble the fruit onto a plate and gently mix through the rose and orange dressing. Scatter with the pistachios and rose petals (if using), and serve warm, with the demerara sugar on the side for an optional sweet hit.

SAFFRON PEARS & RHUBARB WITH RICOTTA

I made this dish for my Dutch publishers on a visit to my flat just before Lockdown 2020 kicked in – so at the time of writing this is a nostalgic dish, as I made it the last time I entertained at home. It's a light, elegant end to a party.

Serves: 4
Prep: 15 minutes
Cook: 10 minutes

1 large pinch of good saffron
  e.g. Belazu
150ml boiling water
150g caster sugar
3 firm, round, ripe pears,
  cut into ½ cm slices
Olive oil, for brushing
12 sticks of rhubarb,
  forced if in season
4 tablespoons ricotta
A handful of toasted hazelnuts
A few fresh mint leaves

First, get your saffron syrup ready: steep your saffron in a couple of tablespoons of the boiling water for 5 minutes, then give it a good mash with the back of a spoon to release the colour and flavour. Tip the saffron water into a small saucepan with the rest of the water and the caster sugar, and heat gently until the sugar has dissolved. Set aside.

Once your barbecue is good and hot, arrange the coals so that one side is a little cooler (see page 11). Brush the sliced pears with a little olive oil, and cook on the cooler end of the barbecue for about 5–6 minutes on each side, until just tender. Repeat with the rhubarb for about 3 minutes per side, taking the fruit over to the hotter side of the barbecue with tongs as needed.

Once both fruits are just cooked through, but still holding their shape, transfer to a shallow roasting tin and cover with the saffron syrup. If you have time, leave them to sit for anything from 10 minutes to an hour.

Serve the fruit in four bowls, with a scoop of ricotta, a handful of toasted hazelnuts and mint leaves to garnish.

THE ELVIS AFTERNOON BARBECUE SANDWICH: CHOCOLATE, PEANUT BUTTER & BANANA

This is unashamedly calorie-loaded. I've given the quantities below for just one sandwich: multiply as needed. Also works well for breakfast.

Serves: 1
Prep: 10 minutes
Cook: 8 minutes

2 thick slices of good white bread
1 tablespoon peanut butter
1 banana, sliced into coins
20g dark vegan chocolate,
 roughly chopped
A pinch of sea salt flakes

Spread one side of the bread with the peanut butter, then top with the banana coins, dark chocolate and a scattering of sea salt flakes. Sandwich with the other piece of bread, and press down.

Once your barbecue is medium hot, grill your sandwich for 2–4 minutes on each side, pressing it down with a spatula, until the bread is toasted to your liking, and serve hot.

Note: If you are vegan or making this for vegans, do make sure to use vegan dark chocolate.

SUMMER PUDDING PACKETS:
VANILLA ROASTED BERRIES
WITH BRIOCHE, MASCARPONE & ALMONDS

This deconstructed spin on a summer pudding (where deconstructed is code for much, much easier) lets you gently cook your fruit in a packet on the barbecue, and toast your brioche alongside. Replace the chilled mascarpone with ice cream, if you wish.

Serves: 4
Prep: 10 minutes
Cook: 10 minutes

150g blackberries
275g raspberries
225g blueberries or grapes
2 teaspoons caster sugar
1 vanilla pod, split
8 slices of brioche
4 tablespoons chilled mascarpone
A handful of toasted almonds
and fresh mint leaves, to serve

Take a large piece of foil and place the blackberries, raspberries and blueberries or grapes in the middle. Scatter over the caster sugar, lay the vanilla pod on top, then fold the foil into a neat parcel, with the seams at the top.

Once your barbecue is medium hot, place the foil packet on one side of the barbecue, and let the berries cook for 10–15 minutes. Meanwhile, toast your sliced brioche in batches on the other side of the barbecue, cutting them into triangles once toasted.

Divide the lightly cooked fruit between four plates, with the toasted brioche. Add a tablespoon of mascarpone, scatter over the toasted almonds and mint leaves, and serve hot.

DULCE DE LECHE PASSIONFRUIT POTS
WITH CHOCOLATE & RICOTTA

I love the combination of passionfruit with chocolate: it works beautifully with dulce de leche in these easy, mildly addictive custard pots. Wheel a plate of these out with coffee after dinner – they're simple to prepare ahead and just flash on the barbecue to finish off.

Serves: 4–6
Prep: 10 minutes
Cook: 15 minutes

8 passionfruit, halved
60g ricotta
2 free-range egg yolks
40g dulce de leche
    (or use tinned caramel)
A pinch of sea salt flakes
30g 70% dark chocolate,
    roughly chopped,
    plus 1 square for grating

Scoop the seeds and flesh from the passionfruit, reserving the shells, and transfer to a bowl with the ricotta, egg yolks, dulce de leche and a pinch of sea salt flakes. Whisk until well incorporated.

Divide the chopped dark chocolate between the empty passionfruit shells, then fill each to the top with the caramel ricotta mixture.

Once your barbecue is medium hot, place the shells on the barbecue, filling side up. Cover with a lid or inverted roasting tin and cook for 10–15 minutes, until the filling has set into a thick custard.

Grate over a little dark chocolate just before serving hot, with teaspoons.

ORANGE FLOWER WATER PEACHES
WITH ROSEMARY, ALMONDS & CREAM

Rosemary, sage, thyme – I love using them in sweet dishes, and particularly with fruit. Here, rosemary combines with lightly griddled peaches and crisp almonds for an easy end to a late-summer party.

Serves: 4
Prep: 10 minutes
Cook: under 20 minutes

3 heaped tablespoons soft light brown sugar
2 sprigs of fresh rosemary, leaves finely chopped
4 just ripe to underripe peaches, halved
40g toasted flaked almonds
2 teaspoons orange flower water
Crème fraîche, to serve

Mix the sugar and rosemary together and set aside on a plate.

Once your barbecue is ready, dip the cut side of the peaches in the rosemary sugar, then grill the peaches cut side up for 5 minutes. Flip them over and grill for a further 5 minutes, keeping a close eye so the sugar caramelises, rather than burns. (Don't worry if you lose a bit of sugar to the grill – the peaches will still caramelise beautifully.)

Remove the hot peaches from the grill and arrange on a platter. Scatter over the flaked almonds, scatter over the orange blossom water, and serve hot with the crème fraîche alongside.

CINNAMON GRIDDLED PINEAPPLE WITH TOASTED COCONUT

At Dinner by Heston Blumenthal, pineapples are slow-cooked whole on a rotating spit – fun to watch, and even more so to eat. You could certainly adapt the recipe below to cook the pineapple peeled and whole, turning it on the barbecue every 5 minutes or so and using the leaves as a handle – for a quicker version, slice it up and brush with this moreish cinnamon sugar glaze.

Serves: 4
Prep: 10 minutes
Cook: 15 minutes

2 tablespoons soft dark brown
   sugar
2 tablespoons water
1 teaspoon ground cinnamon
1 large pineapple, peeled, cored
   and cut into eighths
1 lime, juice only
A handful of toasted coconut flakes
   and fresh mint leaves, to serve

Mix the dark brown sugar, water and cinnamon together, and set aside.

Once your barbecue is medium hot, grill the pineapple for 3–4 minutes on each side, until starting to catch. Brush generously with the cinnamon sugar mixture, then grill for a further 2 minutes or so on each side, until caramelised.

Arrange the pineapple on a platter and squeeze over the lime juice. Scatter over the toasted coconut flakes and mint leaves, and serve hot.

HONEY & ORANGE GRIDDLED PAPAYA WITH MINT

A simple and refreshing end to a barbecue, with a nice citrus kick. Serve with teaspoons, to scoop out the insides as with a kiwi fruit. I love the flavours you get from cooking half the citrus marinade on the barbecue, and leaving the rest as a fresh dressing to finish.

Serves: 4
Prep: 10 minutes
Cook: 15 minutes

3 tablespoons olive or coconut oil
3 tablespoons honey
½ orange, juice and zest
1 lime, juice and zest
2 just ripe papayas, quartered,
   seeds removed
A handful of fresh mint leaves,
   to serve

Mix the olive or coconut oil, honey, orange and lime juice and zest together, and brush half over the cut sides of the papaya. Reserve the remaining mixture, and set aside.

Once your barbecue is good and hot, cook the papaya cut side up for 5 minutes. Then flip and cook for another 3–5 minutes, until the sugars caramelise.

Pour the dressing over the hot papaya quarters, and scatter over the fresh mint leaves before serving.

Note: To veganise, substitute maple syrup for the honey.

WHAT TO DO WITH YOUR LEFTOVERS

WHAT TO DO WITH YOUR LEFTOVERS

BUILD A BANH MI

MAKE A RICE OR NOODLE BOWL

STIR IT THROUGH PASTA

MAKE IT BREAKFAST

BUILD A BANH MI (VIETNAMESE BAGUETTE)

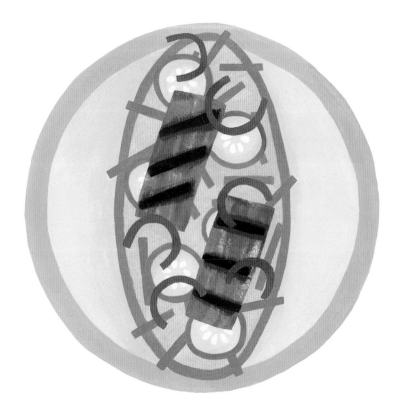

Grab yourself a baguette, some crisp, cold shredded carrots, cucumber and coriander (pickled mooli optional) and build yourself the classic Vietnamese banh mi. Usually stuffed with marinated tofu or tempeh when vegetarian, you could equally use any of the follwing leftovers:

CHARRED ASPARAGUS WITH CHILLI,
PEANUTS & COCONUT

GRIDDLED PAPAYA WITH TAMARIND,
CHILLI & COCONUT

SRIRACHA GRIDDLED TOFU
WITH SPRING ONIONS, LIME & CORIANDER)

VIETNAMESE GRIDDLED TOFU
WITH TOMATOES & SPRING ONIONS

MAKE A RICE OR NOODLE BOWL

With leftovers from the recipes below, build yourself a Korean-inspired bibimbap bowl of rice with colourful toppings, or use to top noodles and broth.

BARBECUED SPROUTS WITH CHILLI,
LEMON & ALMONDS

CRISPY GINGER-CAULIFLOWER WINGS
WITH TAMARIND & CORIANDER

GUNPOWDER POTATOES WITH FENNEL SEEDS,
CHILLI, CORIANDER & CASHEWS

SPICED PANEER WITH GRIDDLED MANGO,
AVOCADO, CHILLI & CORIANDER

PANEER WITH HARISSA, GRIDDLED GREEN BEANS,
CHICKPEAS & LIME

STIR IT THROUGH PASTA

The recipes below work beautifully chopped into bite-sized pieces, then stirred through a bowl of linguine or spaghetti for a hot lunch, or penne, fusilli or macaroni for the perfect lunchbox salad – just add along a little good olive oil.

RED PEPPER, FETA, BASIL & PINE NUT BURGERS

SIMPLE SAGE & ONION CANNELLINI BURGERS

GRIDDLED PORTOBELLO MUSHROOMS
& LEEKS WITH TARRAGON & WALNUTS

RICOTTA WITH GRIDDLED SQUASH, CHARD,
HONEY & HAZELNUTS

GRIDDLED ASPARAGUS, RADISHES & BURRATA
WITH LEMON & BASIL

MAKE IT BREAKFAST

Leftover griddled fruit makes an excellent topping for porridge, granola with yogurt or French toast. Use up the following:

HONEY & ORANGE GRIDDLED PAPAYA
WITH MINT

SIMPLY ROASTED APRICOTS WITH ROSE
& PISTACHIO

CINNAMON GRIDDLED PINEAPPLE
WITH TOASTED COCONUT

ORANGE FLOWER WATER PEACHES
WITH ROSEMARY, ALMONDS & CREAM

SUMMER PUDDING PACKETS: VANILLA ROASTED BERRIES
WITH TOASTED BRIOCHE, MASCARPONE & ALMONDS

GRIDDLED CHERRIES WITH WARM GOAT'S CHEESE,
MINT & WALNUTS (USE TO TOP BUTTERED MUFFINS
OR SAVOURY FRENCH TOAST)

INDEX

ABOUT THE AUTHOR

Rukmini Iyer is the bestselling author of the *Roasting Tin* series. She is a recipe writer, food stylist and formerly a lawyer. She loves creating delicious and easy recipes with minimum fuss and maximum flavour. Rukmini believes family dinners are an integral part of the day and is passionate about helping people make it possible.

Rukmini grew up in Cambridgeshire with the best of three food cultures: Bengali and South Indian food from her parents' Indian heritage, along with classic 80s mac & cheese, sponge puddings and cheese & pineapple on sticks. Rukmini's career began with a training contract at a leading law firm, but she realised that as she spent all day thinking about food, all evening cooking, and most of her law lectures or time in the office scribbling down ideas for new dishes in the margins of her notebook, a career in food was a sensible move. She decided to retrain as a food stylist, so after cookery school and a summer working at a Michelin-starred restaurant to learn the ropes, she began work as a food stylist. Surrounded by food all day on photo shoots, she noticed the meals she made at home grew simpler, often just in a roasting tin, and that there were ways of packing in flavour and interest to the dishes with an absolute minimum effort – this became the inspiration for the series.

As well as writing cookbooks, Rukmini styles and writes recipes for numerous brands and publications, including Waitrose, *The Guardian* and Fortnum & Mason. When not working with food, she can usually be found walking her beautiful border collie Pepper by the riverside in East London, entertaining at home or filling her balcony and flat with more plants than they can hold. Rukmini runs an occasional series of supper clubs for charities including Oxfam and Women's Aid.

@ missminifer   @ missminifer

ACKNOWLEDGEMENTS

The idea for a vegetarian barbecue book came from *The Roasting Tin* series editor, Rowan Yapp, and I'd like to thank her for her continued support and friendship, now from across the river at Bloomsbury. Thanks to Felicity Blunt for her wonderful agenting and presence, to Mireille Harper, Tamsin English and Rachel Cugnoni for taking over the reins in editing and cajoling text from me, to Sarah Bennie and Kate Neilan for brilliant PR and marketing, and to the whole team at Vintage for cheerleading.

Pene Parker thank you once again for your incredible art direction and design, and to David Loftus for your stunning photography – this is, I think, my favourite out of all the books: I reckon you can tell from looking at it how much we all enjoyed working on it together. Rachel, thank you for lending us your beautiful garden and house to work from: my new goal is to create a similar herbaceous border (and then dissuade the border collie from wrecking it.) Jo Jackson, thank you for your brilliant help on and around the shoot – my food always tastes better when you make it. And Tamsin, you were a legend on shoot and so much fun to work with – I do promise to reply to emails if you agree to do more books with us . . . !

Grace Helmer, your illustrations are as always so beautiful, I would – and do – have them up on my wall at home, and I'm delighted that you've done such lovely work on this book as with the *Roasting Tin* series.

Pippa Leon and Jo Jackson, thank you both for considered, thoughtful recipe testing – I very much appreciated having you for second opinions for the book.

To my friends and family, thank you for your love and support always – Danielle, Emma, Christine, Laura, Rosie, Ruby – what a team to have. Padz, mi hermana (pesce) vegetariana – I hope this book opens lots of interesting new barbecue possibilities for you, and Mum and Dad, thank you for lending me the garden to test the book – it was lovely to cook so many dishes for you and get helpful feedback on the recipes and fire-building. (Not sure if Pepper stealing paneer kofte counts as helpful feedback, but they are one of my favourite dishes in the book, so she shows excellent taste – thanks, Principessa.)

10 9 8 7 6 5 4 3 2

Square Peg, an imprint of Vintage,
20 Vauxhall Bridge Road,
London SW1V 2SA

Square Peg is part of the Penguin Random House group
of companies whose addresses can be found at:
global.penguinrandomhouse.com.
Text copyright © Rukmini Iyer 2021

Rukmini Iyer has asserted her right to be identified as
the author of this Work in accordance with the Copyright,
Designs and Patents Act 1988

First published by Square Peg in 2021
Penguin.co.uk/vintage

A CIP catalogue record for this book is available
from the British Library
ISBN 9781529110272

Design & prop styling by Pene Parker
Photography by David Loftus
Illustrations by Grace Helmer
Food styling by Rukmini Iyer
Food styling assistance by Jo Jackson
Recipe testing by Pippa Leon and Jo Jackson

Printed and bound by L.e.g.o. S.p.A.

THE ROASTING TIN SERIES

THE ROASTING TIN
SIMPLE ONE DISH DINNERS

RUKMINI IYER

THE GREEN ROASTING TIN
VEGAN & VEGETARIAN ONE DISH DINNERS

RUKMINI IYER

THE QUICK ROASTING TIN
30 MINUTE ONE DISH DINNERS

RUKMINI IYER

THE ROASTING TIN AROUND THE WORLD
GLOBAL ONE DISH DINNERS

RUKMINI IYER

AVAILABLE NOW